English *for* CUSTOMER CARE

SHORT COURSE SERIES

Rosemary Richey

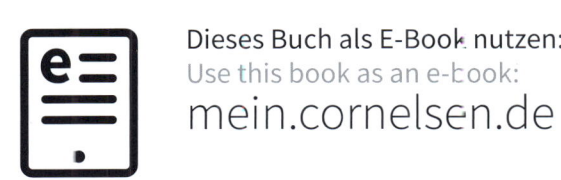

Dieses Buch als E-Book nutzen:
Use this book as an e-book:
mein.cornelsen.de

Impressum

Verfasserin:	Rosemary Richey, München
Berater/in:	Clive Dennis, Berlin
	Britta Landermann, Steinhagen
Projektleitung:	Sylee Gore
Außenredaktion und Koordination:	Stacy Dorgan Bentz
Redaktionelle Mitarbeit:	James Copeland, Meike Kolle
Bildredaktion:	Meike Kolle
Layoutkonzept:	finedesign, Berlin
Technische Umsetzung:	zweiband.media, Berlin
Umschlagsgestaltung:	Jan Haux / Pepe Jürgens, Berlin

www.cornelsen.de

2. Auflage, 1. Druck 2022

Basierend auf English for Customer Care ISBN 978-3-464-01882-8

Alle Drucke dieser Auflage sind inhaltlich unverändert und können im Unterricht nebeneinander verwendet werden.

© 2015 Cornelsen Schulverlage GmbH, Berlin
© 2022 Cornelsen Verlag GmbH, Berlin

Druck: Athesiadruck GmbH

ISBN: 978-3-464-20337-8

PEFC zertifiziert
Dieses Produkt stammt aus nachhaltig bewirtschafteten Wäldern und kontrollierten Quellen.
www.pefc.de
PEFC/18-31-166

Table of Contents

Introducing *English for Customer Care*

The ability to communicate well in English is essential for finding and maintaining a profitable customer base worldwide. It requires the effective use of language and skills in face-to-face meetings, telephoning, and writing. *English for Customer Care* is your guide to successful customer service in English.

- The book's seven units cover the most common topics, language, and skills needed in customer care. The Table of Contents on page 3 provides a broad overview of the material in the book.

- The units build on scenarios in which employees communicate with customers. A wide range of exercises allows you to put the skills and phrases you've learned into practice.

- The simulations found in each unit provide an opportunity for you to use your new skills and language in situations relevant to your professional life.

- Listening exercises in each unit, found on the accompanying CD, expand upon and enhance the realistic scenarios introduced in the units. They feature a broad range of accents to help you practice your listening skills and prepare for the way English is spoken as a global lingua franca in business.

- The book encourages regular discussion with other people in your English course. The discussion exercises give you the opportunity to draw on aspects of your personal experience while practicing key language.

- In the back of the book you will find Phrases to Use, a comprehensive list of useful phrases to refer to when completing communicative exercises or in your professional life. Transcripts for the listening activities, an Answer Key, and an A–Z Wordlist are also provided to assist you as you work through the book.

The Needs Analysis on the next page will help you get started with the book by supporting you in setting personal learning goals and assessing your progress once you have worked through the material in the book.

I hope you enjoy using the book as you build your confidence in working with customers in English.

Rosemary Richey

Needs Analysis

English for Customer Care is designed to improve your ability to communicate effectively with customers in English. However, you are in the best position to know what language and skills you need to develop most to help you in your work.

Look at the lists below and spend a few minutes ticking the items that you consider most important. Which do you want to prioritize and improve? Add other items to the lists that you would like to concentrate on.

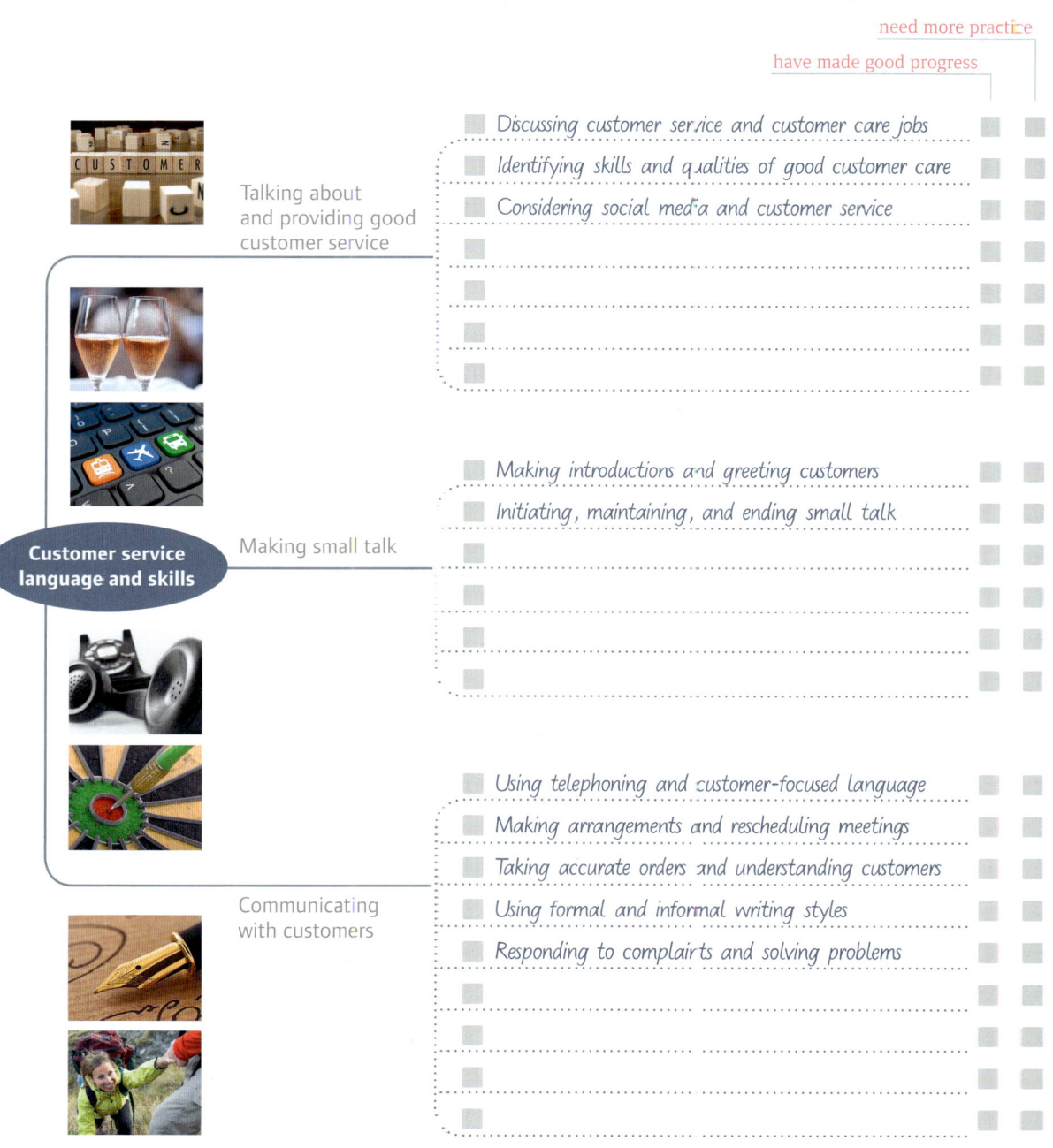

need more practice

have made good progress

Talking about and providing good customer service

- Discussing customer service and customer care jobs
- Identifying skills and qualities of good customer care
- Considering social media and customer service

Customer service language and skills

Making small talk

- Making introductions and greeting customers
- Initiating, maintaining, and ending small talk

Communicating with customers

- Using telephoning and customer-focused language
- Making arrangements and rescheduling meetings
- Taking accurate orders and understanding customers
- Using formal and informal writing styles
- Responding to complaints and solving problems

Try to keep the language and skills you want to improve in mind while working with the book. Once you have completed it, turn back to this page and assess your progress.

CUSTOMER

1 Customer Care Essentials

Customer care is a top priority for almost any business nowadays. Which companies do you think give the best customer service? Write down two or three examples. Why do you think these companies give superior service? Search the internet on your phone or laptop for the latest ranking. How does your list compare?

Companies with the best customer service	Reasons why

 Discuss your answers in small groups.

1 Read about Amazon, a leader in customer service. Then make a list of reasons for its success.

Amazon.com is one the most successful companies on the internet. It uses and develops the latest web-based technologies. However, the company is especially well known for the quality and consistency of its customer service.

Compared to other major companies, Amazon typically ranks top in customer satisfaction. How does it manage this? The company makes shopping online simple and convenient. Customers can easily find everything they need to shop Amazon's large product range, make inquiries, and track orders Even returning products is an easy and efficient procedure.

According to feedback from customer surveys, Amazon scores the best in "experience ratings." This rating system focuses on customer trust, forgiveness in the case of complaints or problems, and the general online experience. Customers give Amazon top marks for online interactions and assistance over the phone. In particular, Amazon rates excellent in meeting the needs of its customers.

"The customer comes first" is an old saying, but it still holds very true for Amazon. The latest website technology is a must, but it does not come before giving high quality customer service. This is an ongoing aim of Amazon. It is how the company maintains its success.

Words you need
complaint Beschwerde
convenient günstig, praktisch
to develop entwickeln
forgiveness Nachsicht, Vergebung
inquiry Anfrage
to maintain aufrechterhalten
product range Sortiment, Produktpalette
to rank rangieren, einen Rang einnehmen
to rate bewerten
to score erzielen
survey Umfrage
to track (nach)verfolgen

up-to-date website technology

....

....

2 Find a word in the text in Exercise 1 that means the same thing as the words below.

1 contentment / happiness   ....

2 target / objective   ....

3 help   ....

4 very good   ....

5 to believe in / to count on   ....

6 something that is easy and uncomplicated   ....

3 Now circle the suitable word to complete each sentence.

1 We like the **convenience | contentment** of Amazon's return policy.
2 I can **maintain | trust** the company to provide good service.
3 When you contact the Amazon helpline, agents offer you friendly **assistance | forgiveness**.
4 Amazon's highest **aim | rating** is to give the best customer service possible.
5 Customer service needs to give total customer **objective | satisfaction**.

4 You are in a meeting with a potential customer. Answer his/her questions about your company with some key vocabulary and phrases from Exercises 1–3.

Q: What makes your company different from your competitors?

A: Our company offers .... [1]. We're especially well known for

.... [2].

Q: How do you make it easy and flexible for the customer?

A: We offer convenient services such as .... [3].

Q: Could you tell me about your customer experience rating?

A: Yes, our customers tell us .... [4].

5 Complete the diagram below with the words from the box.

cashier · clerk · hotel · order entry clerk · receptionist · restaurant · sales · sales assistant

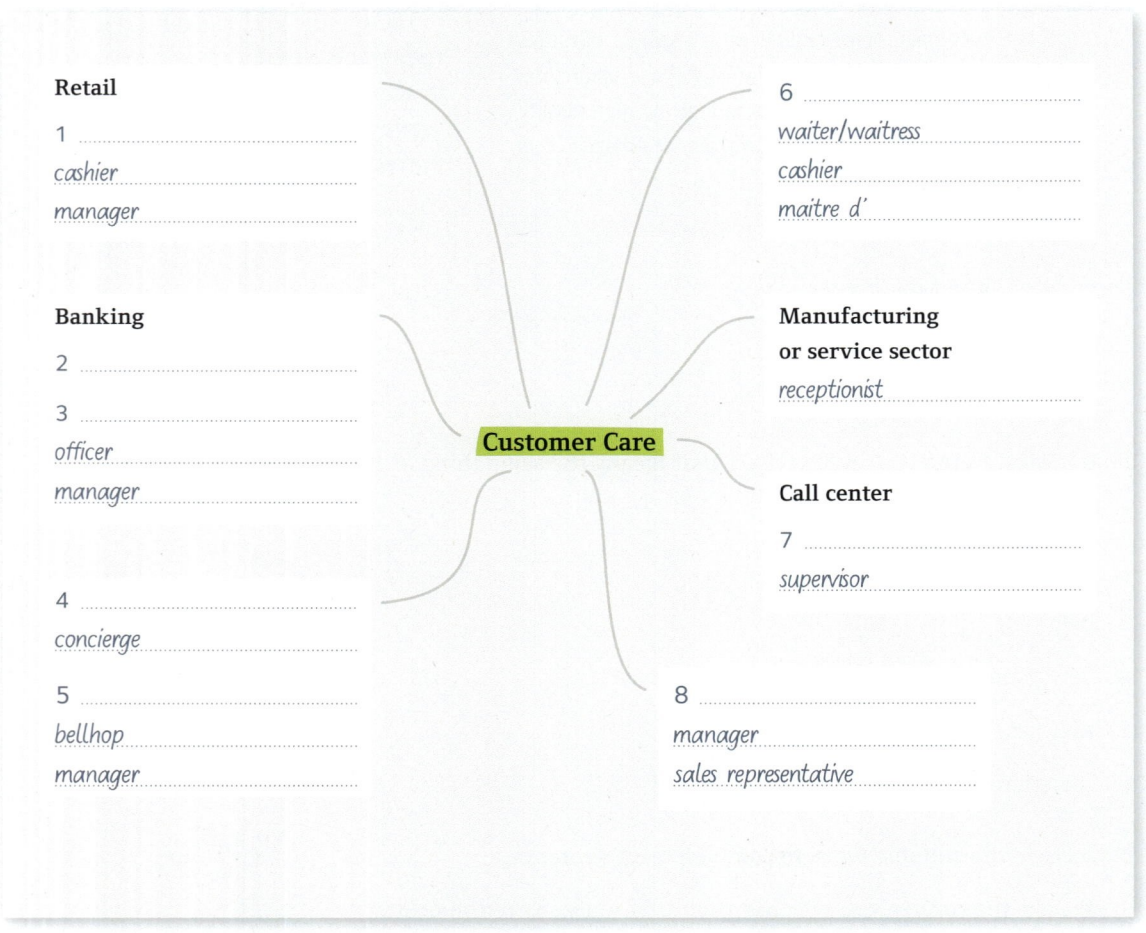

Retail

1 ....

cashier

manager

Banking

2 ....

3 ....

officer

manager

4 ....

concierge

5 ....

bellhop

manager

Customer Care

6 ....

waiter/waitress

cashier

maitre d'

Manufacturing or service sector

receptionist

Call center

7 ....

supervisor

8 ....

manager

sales representative

Is your job or business area on the diagram? If not, add it. Have you had other customer care positions in your company? What kind of jobs in customer service do you prefer?

6 Match the sentence halves about customer care jobs.

1 ☐ Hotel employees deal with ...
2 ☐ People who work in sales take care of ...
3 ☐ Managers at a bank are in charge of ...
4 ☐ Call centers handle ...
5 ☐ Restaurant staff are responsible for ...

a new products and services for new or existing customers
b financial services for customers.
c questions about tourist information from guests.
d providing food and table service for customers.
e customer problems and complaints.

> **Words you need**
>
> **to be in charge of s.o./sth.** Verantwortung für jmd./etw. tragen
> **to be responsible for (doing) sth.** für etw. zuständig sein
> **to deal with sth.** (sich) mit etw. befassen/auseinandersetzen
> **to handle sth.** (sich) mit etw. befassen, etw. handhaben
> **to take care of s.o./sth.** (sich) um jmd./etw. kümmern

7 What do you do in your customer service job? Complete the box with your own job responsibilities.

In my customer care job, I ...
1 take care of ....
2 deal with ....
3 am responsible for ....
4 am in charge of ....

👥 Ask a partner about his or her customer service job.
Use the phrases from the box for your questions.

> What are you responsible for in your job?

8 ◁02 Listen to an excerpt from a Human Resources (HR) manager's talk about customer care jobs. Complete the talk with the words you hear.

For any customer care job at our company, you must be .... [1] in German and English and have a very good telephone .... [2] and excellent customer service skills. .... [3], as well as good .... [4] skills, are essential.

Not only that, it's really important to be able to .... [5] and to show good .... [6].

At any time, really, our customer care employees have to provide customers with first-class service – in all kinds of communications. A customer care agent can .... [7] and .... [8] problems and .... [9]. Superior .... [10] and speaking skills are a must in our customer service jobs.

We also need people who can manage a lot of .... [11] – both internally and externally at our company. This requires clear communication skills with both colleagues and customers. Throughout any contact, the person must show .... [12] and diplomacy.

Listen again to check your answers.

Words you need
follow-through etw. zu Ende führen
manner Art, Weise
to provide bieten
to require benötigen, erfordern
tact Taktgefühl

9 Now complete this list of skills and qualities from the HR manager's talk.

People skills	Business skills
1 good on the telephone	1 work well with a computer
2	2
3	3
4	4
5	5

Which skills are most important for your job? Can you add any others to the lists? Compare answers with a partner.

10 ◁ 03 **Listen to the comments from customer surveys. Mark each comment as positive (P) or negative (N).**

1 ▢ Your company employees are impatient. They never wait for people to finish what they have to say.

> Customer service requires good people skills. These interpersonal skills help you work well with your colleagues. They also assist in socializing with customers and making them feel comfortable.

2 ▢ The customer service agents are always polite and friendly. They always take time to help me and answer my questions.

3 ▢ Why aren't your secretaries more attentive on the phone? They don't listen, and they aren't interested in customers at all.

4 ▢ Your call center agents are really helpful and efficient.

5 ▢ The hotel concierge is very knowledgeable about sightseeing information.

6 ▢ Your colleague was inefficient and seemed to take a long time to process my order.

7 ▢ The clerk was really rude and acted like he didn't see me.

8 ▢ The waiter was well informed about the menu and brought our food fast.

9 ▢ The employees at the reception desk were inattentive and made me wait to be checked in.

10 ▢ The call center agent was very patient and explained everything to me again.

👥 What are the customers' tones of voice like in the positive and negative comments? Have you had similar customer service experiences with banks, call centers, or hotels? Discuss your answers with a partner.

11 **Match the positive adjectives with their negative opposites.**

1 ▢	polite	a	inattentive
2 ▢	patient	b	inefficient
3 ▢	attentive	c	rude
4 ▢	knowledgeable	c	uninformed
5 ▢	efficient	e	impatient

12 Complete the tip box with suitable words.

A Positive Image for Your Company

1 Always be .... and friendly. If you are rude and unfriendly, our customers will go to the competitor.

2 Be .... , so that you hear all the information you need to answer the customers' questions.

3 Answer questions from the customers and deal with transactions quickly and carefully.

   Be ....

4 Be .... about our products and services. Employees who don't understand what we sell make a bad impression.

5 Sometimes it takes time for our customers to understand our products and services.

   Be .... and let them ask as many questions as needed.

---

13 Can you think of adjectives to describe a good image for your company? Complete the list with other adjectives and their opposites.

Good customer service adjectives	Opposites
1	1 ....
2	2 ....
3	3 ....

14

Simulation

👥 **Discuss your customer care profile with a partner. Can you tell your partner something about your job that he/she doesn't know?**

Use the form on the right to prepare yourself.

People skills: With customers I am …

1 *friendly* ....

2 ....

3 ....

4 ....

Business skills: I can …

1 *organize meetings* ....

2 ....

3 ....

4 ....

Customer Care Is an Attitude

Imagine that a customer service representative says the right things and takes care of a transaction or an order really well. But what if the agent speaks with an air of indifference? Are tech skills and efficiency really enough to do a customer care job? Absolutely not! Customer care means
5 so much more than that. People expect to be treated with courtesy and respect. Only a customer service attitude plus know-how can deliver total customer satisfaction for your company.

Some tools for improving customer service attitude are:

- **positive language:**   being friendly, helpful, and tactful
10 - **good listening skills:**   being focused and paying attention to details
- **confirming satisfaction:**   closing the transaction by making sure the customers' needs have been met

A sincere willingness to help the customer will make a big difference to the customer, even if the agent may lack a few skills. The customer care attitude will help you keep your repeat business!

15 At the end of the day, customers can walk away from the transaction knowing they received superior service. This is a true sign of success for the company and customers alike.

> **Words you need**
>
> **air of indifference**
>   gleichgültiges Auftreten
> **attitude** Einstellung
> **courtesy** Höflichkeit
> **efficiency** Effizienz
> **repeat business**
>   Folgegeschäft
> **sincere** aufrichtig
> **transaction** Geschäft,
>   Transaktion

Over to you

- What is your strongest quality in dealing with customers?
- How could you build on your own customer service attitude?
- What sort of training does your company offer to support a good customer care attitude and improvements in skills?

2 Basic Socializing with Customers

In this unit you will …

• welcome customers and introduce yourself and others for the first time
• greet customers you've met in person before
• offer hospitality
• initiate, maintain, and end small talk

How do you feel about socializing with customers in English? Read the small talk survey and decide whether you agree (A) or disagree (D) with each statement.

Making small talk in English

1 ☐ I enjoy making small talk with my customers.

2 ☐ I feel comfortable starting up small talk with new customers.

3 ☐ Sometimes I don't know how to keep small talk with my customers going.

4 ☐ I know which small talk topics to use with my customers.

5 ☐ I use the same small talk topics with all international customers.

6 ☐ I think small talk in English goes on too long. I prefer to make it as short as possible.

Discuss your answers with a partner. On which points do you agree and disagree? Why?

1 What do you usually do when a customer visits your company? Write down some steps on how you'd welcome a customer.

1 *The customer comes to the reception desk.*
2 *I pick up the customer at reception and take him/her to my office or a meeting room.*
3 ....
4 ....
5 ....

Compare procedures with a partner.

Did you know?

It's common in British and American business culture to use first names among colleagues and partners, but this isn't always true in customer care situations. When speaking with a customer, it's always best to use the last name. Or, if you aren't sure which name to use, ask the customer what he/she prefers: "Would you prefer me to use your first or last name?"

2 Label each list of first greetings with a suitable heading from the box.

Greeting the customer · Saying the name of your colleague ·
Saying your name and meeting for the first time

A ....

Welcome to …
I'd like to welcome you to …
We're pleased/delighted to welcome you to …
We're glad/happy to have you here …

B ....

My name's …
Let me introduce myself. I'm … I'm head of sales.
How do you do?
How are you?
We haven't met. I'm …

C ....

I'd like to introduce you to … She's in charge of
    customer service.
Have you met? …, this is …
Let me introduce you to …

> **Words you need**
>
> **delighted** erfreut
> **to introduce** vorstellen

*In formal situations use higher level words such as pleased or delighted.
In comparison, glad or happy would be informal.*

3 Match the greetings to the responses.

1 ▢ We're happy to have you here.
2 ▢ How do you do?
3 ▢ Let me introduce myself. I'm … I'm head of sales.
4 ▢ Have you met? …, this is …
5 ▢ How are you?

a How do you do?
b Nice to meet you. My name's … I'm in advertising.
c Oh, no, we haven't. So nice to meet you.
d Thanks, I'm glad to be here, too.
e Fine, thanks, and you?

> **Did you know?**
>
> "How do you do?" is used in some regions of the US and in some formal settings. It is a first-time greeting. The answer can simply be "How do you do?" or "Nice to meet you." Do not use it when you know the person already.

🔊 04 Listen to check your answers.

4 Practice making these introductions with a partner. Then change partners and try them again.

1 You are at a company party. You see someone you would like to meet. Introduce yourself.
2 Welcome a new customer to your company. Introduce him/her to your colleagues.

> **Did you know?**
>
> Americans tend to say "How are you?" as a greeting. It's not a literal question that requires a detailed answer. A polite answer would be "Fine, thank you. And you?"

> Here are some model greetings to use when you've been in contact with someone via email or telephone but never met in person:
>
> A: Oh, you must be John Andrews!
> B: Oh, hello Bob! Yes, you're right. It's great to meet you finally in person.
> A: It's nice to put a face to the emails and phone calls.
> B: Yes, it sure is. I feel I already know you …

5 Correct the mistakes in the greetings you would use with customers you've met before or know well.

1 How do you do? ....

2 Grate to see you again! ....

3 How are things doing? ....

4 How's about business? ....

> *When greeting a customer you already know, say, "Nice to see you again," not "Nice to meet you again."*

6 Practice making these introductions with a partner. Then change partners and try them again.

1 You're meeting a customer face-to-face for the first time after many emails. Greet him/her.
2 You see a customer you've known for two years. Greet him/her.

> We mostly use contractions (such as *he's* instead of *he is* and *isn't* instead of *is not*) when speaking, both in formal and informal business situations. We sometimes use longer forms instead of contractions in key sentences to make our point or an idea stronger. In rare cases you would use longer forms in conversation if you were to meet a very high-ranking or important person, like a president, Queen Elizabeth, or the Pope.

7 ◁ 05 Listen to someone offering hospitality to a customer. Fill in the missing words or phrases you hear.

A: .... [1] you .... [2] to come this way? Our meeting room is just

down the .... [3].

B: Fine, ... [4] you.

A: .... [5] I .... [6] your coat? .... [7] it on the

.... [8] for you.

B: .... [9], that'd be very kind of you.

A: Please .... [10] a seat. .... [11] I bring you a cup of coffee or tea?

B: Oh, coffee .... [12] fine.

A: How do you .... [13] your coffee?

B: .... [14] black, please.

Words you need

coatrack Garderobe
corridor Gang, Flur

 Listen again to check your answers. Then practice the dialogue with a partner.

What are some other ways you can offer hospitality to customers? What else can you offer to drink when a customer visits your company?

> 1 *Let me* is a common way of offering to help or do something for someone.
> 2 Modal verbs such as *would like*, *could*, and *may* give a base for professional, polite language in all forms of business communication.
> 3 Use *I'll* for spontaneous offers: "I'll bring you a coffee," not "I bring you a coffee."

8 Travel, accommodation, and weather are safe topics for small talk in almost any culture.
Sort the travel words to complete the diagram.

> drive · flight · punctual · traffic jam · trip · turbulence

1 ....

2 ....

service ....

3 ....

4 ....

dining car ....

5 ....

6 ....

highway ....

9 Circle the suitable words for travel small talk questions and answers.

1 Q: How was your **cruise | drive | flight**[1]?
   A: It was fine. Luckily, there weren't any **traffic | car | driving**[2] jams.

2 Q: Did you have a good **travel | flight | excursion**[3]?
   A: Yes, it was very smooth with no **turbulence | trouble | transport**[4].

3 Q: How was your train **trip | drive | tour**[5]?
   A: Really good. I thought we'd have delays because of the weather, but it was **timely | late | punctual**[6].

> public transportation = subway, bus, street car
> vacation travel = tour, excursion, cruise

> We use the verb *drive* only for cars, not for any other form of travel. *Drive* always means you operate a car, so it's not necessary to include *by car* in your sentence.
> "I drive to work every day," not "I drive by car to work every day."
> With other forms of travel, use verbs like *take* or *come.*
> "I took the train to Berlin," not "I drove with the train to Berlin."
> "I'm coming to the meeting by subway," not "I'm driving to the meeting by subway."

10 Match the questions and answers about a customer's accommodation.

1 ☐ Where are you staying?
2 ☐ How's your hotel?
3 ☐ Do you have a room with a view?
4 ☐ Is the hotel in a convenient location?
5 ☐ How's the breakfast buffet?

a It's very comfortable, and the service is excellent.
b Definitely. It's directly on the main pedestrian shopping zone.
c Delicious! They offer just about anything you could want to eat.
d Yes, the room is very nice. It overlooks Marienplatz.
e I've got a room at the Hotel Excelsior.

What other kinds of accommodation could a customer have other than a hotel?

> *What's it like?* is a request for a description about something.

> **Words you need**
>
> **accommodation** Unterkunft
> **definitely** definitiv
> **delicious** lecker, delikat
> **to overlook** überblicken
> **pedestrian** Fußgänger/in

11 Complete the questions and answers about weather using words from the box.

> bothers · find · like · pleasant · stand · uncomfortable

Q: How do you _____[1] the weather today?

A: It's really a _____[2] day to be outdoors.

Q: What was the weather _____[3] when you left New York?

A: It was so _____[4], very rainy and cold.

Q: What kind of weather _____[5] you the most?

A: I really can't _____[6] wind. I normally work in Chicago, where unfortunately it's often windy.

> Weather is a good prompt for talking about the customer's favorite seasons.
> Look at the following topic flow:
> seasons → sports → famous/popular players and teams

12 Ask a partner three small talk questions about his/her last business trip or vacation. Use topics like travel, accommodation, and weather. Then change partners and ask the questions again.

13 Small talk can be made during coffee breaks – or later at lunch, during dinner, or while having drinks. Complete the conversation bubbles with the words and phrases in the box.

> cellars · cuisine · do you do · enjoy · ever · familiar · grew up · internship ·
> join · line of business · originally · recommend · was born

A: Where are you from _____[1]?

B: I _____[2] and _____[3] in Houston, Texas.

C: So, how did you get into this _____[4]?

D: I did an _____[5] program at …

E: What _____[6] in your free time?

F: I _____[7] playing tennis and going to classical music concerts.

G: Have you .... [8]
been to Vienna before?

H: Well, I've been to Austria twice, but I'm not really .... [9] with Vienna.

I: Have you tried our local
.... [10]?

J: Yes, but I only know Wienerschnitzel and Apfelstrudel. What else can you
.... [11] for me to try?

K: Would you like to
.... [12] us for drinks after the meeting?

L: Yes, I'd love to. Could we go to one of your famous wine .... [13]? I've heard you've got very good white wine.

Words you need

internship Praktikum, Praxissemester
familiar bekannt, vertraut
to grow up aufwachsen
line of business Branche
originally ursprünglich
to recommend empfehlen

◁ 06 **Listen to check your answers.**

Use the present perfect to ask about experience.
"Have you been to Berlin before?" not "Were you in Berlin before?"

Use the simple present form of to do for regular activities.
"What do you do at work every day?" not "What are you doing at work every day?"

14 **Sort these topics into the table as either good or taboo for small talk.**

accommodation · age · current news headlines · customers job · free time activities ·
health · home town or country · money · politics · religion · sex · someone's
weight · travel · weather

Good	Taboo

Can you add any other example topics? What is wrong with the taboo topics? Are they taboo in all business small talk situations? Are they taboo in every culture?

Words you need

current aktuell
weight Gewicht

Simulation

Think of a professional situation in which you need to make small talk. Ask a partner three good small talk questions.

Use the form on the right to prepare yourself. How could the small talk develop? After asking each question, try to keep the small talk flowing.

Topic 1: ....

Question: ....

....

Topic 2: ....

Question: ....

....

Topic 3: ....

Question: ....

....

---

16 Circle the correct words for ending small talk with customers.

1 Thanks so much for **traveling | coming**.
2 It was a **pleasure | pleasant** to meet you.
3 Look **ahead | forward** to seeing you again next week.

4 Please **hold | keep** in touch.
5 Goodbye. **Take | Be** care.
6 **Have | Make** a good flight.

---

17 What would you say? Complete the flow chart to review basic socializing and small talk.

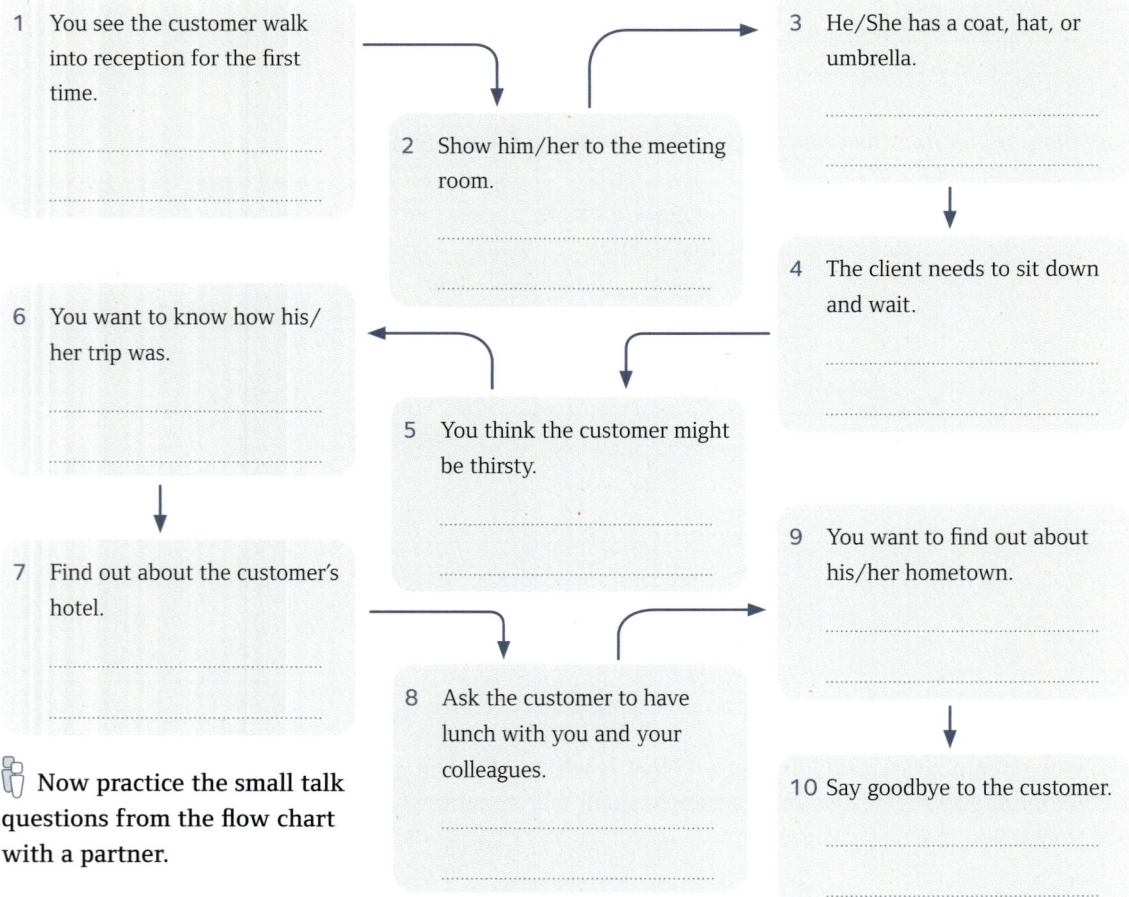

1 You see the customer walk into reception for the first time.
....
....

2 Show him/her to the meeting room.
....
....

3 He/She has a coat, hat, or umbrella.
....
....

4 The client needs to sit down and wait.
....
....

6 You want to know how his/her trip was.
....
....

5 You think the customer might be thirsty.
....
....

7 Find out about the customer's hotel.
....
....

9 You want to find out about his/her hometown.
....
....

8 Ask the customer to have lunch with you and your colleagues.
....
....

10 Say goodbye to the customer.
....
....

Now practice the small talk questions from the flow chart with a partner.

Small Talk Can Make a Big Difference

Many people get impatient with small talk. Someone could say:

"Hot enough for you today?" … "Yes." Or "Too much rain this summer, don't you think?" … "Oh, sure." What you'd really like to say is "Who cares? I can't do anything about it!"

5 What's the point of it all anyway? Why don't we just ride the elevator with our mouths shut or drink our coffee in peace during the breaks in a meeting? Like it or not, small talk is where it all starts in business. If you want to get somewhere 10 with your customers, the first step begins with small talk. There's no guarantee that small talk will make everything go according to plan. Like almost everything else in business, it's a definite risk but still a necessary start.

15 Small talk can have its benefits for us as well. Recent studies suggest that friendly, social interaction can increase our ability to solve problems. As for understanding customers, psychologists claim, "Some social interactions 20 give people a chance to try to read others' minds and get their perspectives on things."

Moreover, light conversation does not just make the customer feel more comfortable, it also makes us feel positive about ourselves as social beings. 25 Whether it be for business or personal reasons, humans just crave connection. That's how Facebook founder Mark Zuckerberg made his multi-billion-dollar fortune. He's proven with Facebook that small talk, while not earth- 30 shattering or highly intellectual, is definitely a lively way to connect to other people.

Perhaps most importantly, your customers will like you more with small talk. As they often say in business, this is a way to make friends and 35 influence people. Customers want to be near people who are generous and confident enough to interact with them. It's simply a sign of respect – and a way to boost your own self-image and confidence.

40 At the end of the day, if you want to have happy customers, keep that small talk going. Stuck? Don't know where to begin? Just look at today's weather forecast!

Words you need
benefit Nutzen, Vorteil
to boost fördern, steigern
confidence Selbstvertrauen
to crave (sich) sehnen nach
earth-shattering weltbewegend
to go according to plan nach Plan verlaufen
to interact interagieren

Over to you

- Do you agree with the author of the article about the benefits of small talk?
- Can you think of any other positive aspects of small talk?
- Which area of small talk could you improve upon with your customers?

In this unit you will …
- use appropriate body language
- learn the language needed for face-to-face encounters with customers
- handle a Q&A session and mingle following a presentation
- socialize at a trade fair

3 Face-to-Face with Customers

Body language can impact any face-to-face encounter with customers. Look at the following examples of good and bad body language. Mark each one positive (P) or negative (N).

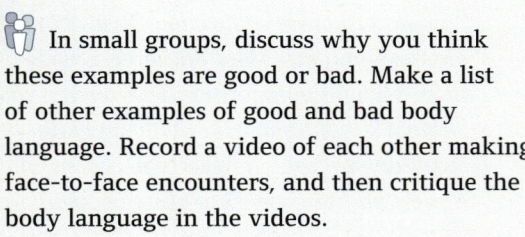

In small groups, discuss why you think these examples are good or bad. Make a list of other examples of good and bad body language. Record a video of each other making face-to-face encounters, and then critique the body language in the videos.

Did you know?

People from different cultures have different understandings of body language. What differences have you experienced with your international customers?

1 Match the meeting steps with the appropriate sentences.

1 ▢ Welcoming a customer
2 ▢ Offering hospitality
3 ▢ Getting down to business
4 ▢ Wrapping up a meeting
5 ▢ Saying goodbye to
   a customer

a Can I offer you something to drink?
b Thanks for coming to the meeting today. It's good to see you (again).
c Could we go over the action points one last time?
d Thanks again for the productive meeting. We'll be in contact again next Friday.
e Shall we get started? As I understand it, you're interested in …

> **Words you need**
>
> **action points** offene Punkte
> **to get down to business** zum Geschäftlichen übergehen
> **to wrap up sth.** etw. beenden

2 ◁07 Listen to the excerpts from a meeting between a sales rep (SR) and a new customer (NC), and write in the missing words.

Welcoming a customer, offering hospitality, and getting down to business

SR: So nice to see you again. Would you like something to drink?
NC: Yes, please. I'll take a black coffee.
SR: So, ...¹ we ....² to business? As I understand from our emails and phone calls, you're interested in our office equipment offers.
NC: Yes, that's right. However, to start, I do have some direct questions about your customer service. Would you ....³ if I asked them now?
SR: Not at all, go ahead.
NC: How will I be able to see that you're keeping your service ....⁴ to us?
SR: Well, that's a really important point. We follow up on customer ....⁵ by regular contact. This means by email, phone, meetings, or even video-conferencing – whichever you prefer.
NC: How often do you ....⁶ your products and services?
SR: We normally ....⁷ our upgrades every six months. We would ....⁸ you of upgrades before providing them to the general market. You would receive special offers on these upgrades.
NC: Thanks for clearing that up. Now I'd really like to take a closer look at your ....⁹ of photocopiers.
SR: All right. I'd be glad to ....¹⁰ that for you.

Wrapping up the meeting and saying goodbye to a customer

SR: So, I think we can ....¹¹ our discussion. We've outlined the products you'd like to order. I'll get them in the contract so you can review the details. Would that be OK?
NC: Yes, that sounds fine.
SR: We'll contact you again by next Monday. Do you use Skype or another type of video link? I could contact you that way, if that's ....¹² for you.
NC: Email is the best way to reach me.
SR: All right, then. Thanks for such a good meeting. Have a nice trip back home!
NC: Thank you for your kind help. Goodbye!

> **Words you need**
>
> **commitment** Verpflichtung
> **to go over sth.** etw. durchsehen
> **to launch** starten, beginnen
> **to mind sth.** etw. dagegen haben
> **sales rep (representative)** Außendienstmitarbeiter/in, Vertreter/in

👥 Listen again to check your answers.
Then practice the dialogue with a partner.

3 Make a list of other customer service questions that can be asked at a meeting. Then practice asking and answering them with a partner.

1 How often do you have upgrades?

2 How do you follow up on customer satisfaction?

3 ....

4 ....

5 ....

4 It's important to conduct small talk during coffee breaks. Write three example small talk questions you can ask a customer. Then practice them with a partner.

1 Where are you from originally? ....

2 ....

3 ....

4 ....

> to mingle = in Kontakt kommen, sich unter die Leute mischen

Question tags such as *aren't you, isn't it, do you,* and *are you* can be used to keep a conversation going.

You're originally from Los Angeles, *aren't you?*
This is your first time in Germany, *isn't it?*
You don't speak Italian, *do you?*
You're not a vegetarian, *are you?*

Signal words can also be used while listening to move the small talk forward.

Oh, really?
How interesting!
Is that so?

> Question tag formula:
> If the main verb is positive, the tag must be negative.
> If the main verb is negative, the tag must be positive.

5 Complete the sentences with the right tag or signal word.

1 You aren't from Zurich, ...?

2 A: I really love cooking.

   B: ....? What kind of food do you like to cook?

3 A: I can speak Spanish.

   B: ....! Where did you learn it?

4 The weather's terrible today,

   ....?

5 Business isn't going very well right now,

   ....?

Practice three questions with tags and listening signal words with a partner.

6 Match the sentence halves to conclude a meeting with a customer.

1 ☐ Let's go over …   a good trip back to New York.
2 ☐ Thanks for …   b a taxi?
3 ☐ Could you contact me … c a productive meeting.
4 ☐ Have a …   d with anything else?
5 ☐ Can I help you …   e our actions points again.
6 ☐ May I call you …   f on Skype next Wednesday?

7 ◁08 After a meeting, the customer may be invited out to a restaurant or just for drinks at a bar or pub. Listen and write in the missing words.

Inviting the customer

A: Would you like to _____¹ us for drinks and dinner?
B: Oh, sure, I'd like that very much.
A: We have a number of good restaurants nearby. What sort of _____² do you prefer?
B: I really like Greek or Mediterranean style food.
A: Great, there's a good Greek restaurant around the corner.

At the restaurant

A: So, what can I _____³ you to drink?
B: _____⁴ a white wine, please.
A: Please order what you'd like for dinner. It's _____⁵ since you're a special customer!
B: Well, I _____⁶ that. I'd like the moussaka and an olive and tomato salad.
A: So, have you had the chance to do any _____⁷ in Munich?
B: Not yet, but I'd really like to see some art museums tomorrow. What do you _____⁸?
A: I highly recommend the Pinakothek Museums. They've got all kinds of art – from the Old Masters to the Expressionists.
B: Sounds fascinating. I think I'll go over there tomorrow morning.

Listen again to check your answers.

> **When ordering in a restaurant, use**
> "I'll have," not "I have"
> "I'd like," not "I want"
> "Could you bring me," not "Bring me."

Words you need
the bill's on us die Rechnung geht auf uns

8 Rewrite the phrases to make them more customer-friendly. Use the audio in Exercise 7 to help you.

1 Want to come to dinner with us? ....

2 How about a drink? ....

3 We're paying the dinner bill. ....

4 Give me a whiskey. ....

5 Bring me a schnitzel and French fries. ....

9 Practice making polite offers at a bar or restaurant with a partner.

Your offer to the customer of food or drink

....

....

....

10 ◁09 Presentations are another important way to show customer care with new or existing customers. Listen to the expert giving advice about the importance of question and answer (Q&A) sessions following presentations. Then decide if the sentences are true or false.

	True	False
1 Giving a presentation always means we can interact with customers well.	☐	☐
2 How one handles the Q&A session in a presentation makes a big difference to customers.	☐	☐
3 A presenter should always answer a customer's question, even if the answer may not be right.	☐	☐
4 Mingling with customers is a chance to hear how they reacted to the presentation.	☐	☐
5 Customers don't notice if the presenter is listening to them or not.	☐	☐

Do you agree with the advice? Why or why not?

11 The question and answer session of a presentation is a good chance to show a customer-friendly attitude. Tick the best sentence to say to a customer in each conversation bubble.

1
- ☐ Your questions are too complicated.
- ☐ Let me try to answer some of your questions.
- ☐ I can't answer your questions completely.

2
- ☐ Could you give me some background on your company?
- ☐ What about your company?
- ☐ I don't know anything about your company.

3
- ☐ I don't deal with that.
- ☐ I don't know about that.
- ☐ I'll look into that for you.

4
- ☐ Could you leave me your business card? Here's my card with my complete contact details.
- ☐ Give me your business card. And here's mine.
- ☐ Don't you have a business card?

- Sign the list, OK?
- Would you mind signing the list?
- Here's the list, so sign it.

- Why don't we get in touch next week?
- I'm going to call you next week.
- Give me a call on Monday.

Making suggestions and asking politely
<u>*Why don't we*</u> *+ verb*
   <u>*Why don't we meet*</u> *next Tuesday?*
<u>*Would you mind*</u> *+ gerund (verb in the <u>ing</u> form that acts like a noun)*
   <u>*Would you mind emailing*</u> *me next week?*

Words you need

to get in touch sich melden, Kontakt aufnehmen

12 Mingling after the presentation is a useful way to get to know customers better.

1
Please help yourself to drinks from the bar and snacks from the Italian buffet.

2
I see on your name tag you are ... from ...

3
So pleased to meet you.

4
How did you find the presentation? Did we offer something that meets your needs? What was lacking, in your opinion?

Think of more small talk questions or starters to use when mingling with a customer. Practice them with a partner.

13 Trade fairs are an excellent networking opportunity for finding new customers. How often do you attend trade fairs? Share your experiences with a partner.

Where ....

Which products or services promoted ....

Customer interaction notes ....

....

14 Complete the sentences said at a trade fair with words from the box.

> ask · brochure · email · enjoying · free ·
> glad · introduce · make sure · mind ·
> particular · put · suitable

Use *would you mind if* + the simple past to ask a question in a polite, indirect manner.
Would you mind if I called you on Monday?

A   I'd like to ....[1] myself. I'm Otto Brandt.
I work for Metro GmbH.
May I ....[2] your name?

B   So, Mr. Gillan, how are you ....[3] the trade fair?

C   Well, then, are you looking for anything in ....[4]?

D   OK, but please feel ....[5] to ask me any questions. I'd be ....[6]
to go over our products and try to find something ....[7] for your company.

E   Ah, can I interest you in our latest ....[8]? It has information about our company
and our full range of products.

F   Would you like to ....[9] your name on our mailing list?

G   Would you ....[10] if I took your business card? I'll ....[11]
you're on our list. And here's my card with full contact details. I'll send you a quick
........................[12] next week to see if I can help you with any of our products.

🔊10 **Listen to check your answers.**

15 Rewrite the following sentences said at trade fairs to make them more polite and friendly.
Use the audio in Exercise 14 to help you.

1   Who are you? ....

2   What are you looking for? ....

3   Ask me a question if you want. ....

4   Do you want a brochure? ....

5   I'll put your name on the mailing list, OK? ....

6   Give me your business card. ....

7   I'll contact you sometime soon. ....

16

Simulation

👥 **Try this trade fair practice with a partner. Then switch roles and practice again.**

Use the language you've learned for face-to-face encounters with customers and socializing at trade fairs.

A   You are at a trade fair to promote your newest product or service. You greet a possible new customer. Ask him/her two or three small talk questions about the trade fair. Offer assistance to him/her at the stand.

B   You're browsing a stand at a trade fair. Introduce yourself to the rep and ask him/her about their latest products and services.

Customer Service Expert

Home | Our Services | Our Customers | Customer Care | Contact

Home | Customer Care

The Art of Listening Carefully

Customer care usually means a lot of talking, but how about more listening instead? Unfortunately, we listen mostly to the sound of our own voices and not nearly enough to the customers.

Listening may be the most important skill needed in business. It means focusing all of our
5 attention on customers. If we don't concentrate on what they're saying, they notice right away!

The best way to alienate your customers is to not listen to them. If you don't listen, you can never learn from them or understand them. Moreover, it damages your business reputation as a customer service professional.

If we listen to our customers, it makes them feel valued and that they are important to our
10 business. It also increases our confidence that we are doing everything possible to take care of the customer from start to finish. This is a necessary foundation for any business relationship.

Here are some guidelines from experts on developing good listening skills:
 – Try to have a genuine interest in the customer.
 – Maintain good eye contact and positive body language.
15 – Notice the customer's tone of voice.
 – Don't interrupt the customer.
 – Listen for ideas, not just words and phrases.
 – Take notes as you are listening.
 – Switch off your own problems.
20 – Think like the customer!

When listening to customers, only speak in order to:
 – ask questions for clarification.
 – repeat key ideas to make sure you know exactly what the customer wants.
25 – summarize what the customer has said in order to show that you follow him/her.
 – answer the customer's questions.

The bottom line is that customers will never have a fully satisfactory experience unless they are confident that you're listening carefully.

Words you need

to alienate vor den Kopf stoßen, abschrecken
clarification Klärung, Verdeutlichung
foundation Basis, Fundament
genuine authentisch, echt
to interrupt unterbrechen
to switch off abschalten

Over to you

· On a scale of 0 to 5, how would you rate your listening skills?
· What's the biggest difficulty for you in listening to customers?
· How could you improve your listening skills?

In this unit you will …
- learn how to make a good impression in English
- practice basic telephoning phrases
- make arrangements
- reschedule a meeting
- build confidence on the phone

4   Managing Customers on the Phone

Customer phone calls are important to any business. Look at the checklist and tick what you normally do on the phone to make a good impression on customers.

1	☐	I answer the phone by the third ring.
2	☐	I begin with a polite greeting.
3	☐	I say my name clearly.
4	☐	I ask for the caller's name (if they haven't identified themselves).
5	☐	I ask the caller to repeat or spell something if it's not clear.
6	☐	I use different phrases throughout the phone call, so I don't sound repetitive and boring.
7	☐	I finish the call by summarizing the details.
8	☐	I ask the customer how he/she would like to be contacted in the future.
9	☐	I thank the caller.
10	☐	I say goodbye in a friendly manner.

Does anything on this list seem unnecessary to you? Can you think of anything that should be added to the list? Compare answers with a partner.

1 ◁11 Listen to two phone calls and say what kind of impression they make. With a partner, discuss what went right and what went wrong in the calls.

Right ....

Wrong ....

Listen to the second call again. How did Martha …

1 … **answer the phone?** Hello, Martha Greer speaking. ....

2 … **say she didn't understand something?** Sorry, could .... ?

3 … **say that there was a mistake?** .... you've got the wrong extension, Mr. Kraft.

4 … **offer help?** .... to connect you?

5 … **end the phone call?** I'm putting you through now. ....

2 🔊 12 Listen to two telephone calls and complete the dialogue with the words you hear.

Call 1

Elke: Good morning, Apex Industries. ....¹?

John: Yes, this is John Richards from Customer Software Services. I'd like to speak to Eva Lang, please.

Elke: Of course, ...², please … Oh, it seems that her line is busy.

Could you hold for a moment? Or ....³ to leave a message?

John: I'd prefer to hold for just a minute or two.

Elke: OK, she'll be with you soon.

Elke: Mr. Richards, ...⁴. I'm putting you through to Ms. Lang's office now. If you get cut off for some reason, please call again

John: I'm sorry. Could you speak up a bit? I didn't ....⁵ that.

Elke: Sure. I'm connecting you now to Ms. Lang's office. If you don't get through, please call again.

Call 2

Elke: Good morning, Apex Industries.

John: This is John Richards again.

....⁶

I got cut off when you tried to put me through.

Elke: I'm ....⁷ about that.

John: I really need to get through to Ms. Lang this afternoon. Could I leave a message for her?

Elke: ....⁸, Mr. Richards. Could I have your phone number?

John: Yes, I'm calling from my cell phone. It's country code +1, then 408 555 3392.

Elke: Right. So, that's country code +1, 408 555 3392. ....⁹ she calls you back today. Can I help you with anything else?

John: Would it be possible to have her cell phone number? Could you perhaps look it up for me?

Elke: Yes, that's ....¹⁰. It's in our directory. It's +49 for Germany, then 152 288 17386.

John: 152 288 17386. Thanks once again. Bye.

Elke: You're welcome. Goodbye

Words you need

to cut off die Verbindung trennen
directory Telefonverzeichnis
extension Durchwahl
to get back to s.o. jmd. antworten
to put through durchstellen
to speak up lauter sprechen

Offering or promising action at the moment
I'll + verb *I'll connect you*, not *I connect you.*

Checking understanding in a polite way
I didn't (quite) catch / get that.
I'm afraid I don't (quite) follow you, not *I don't understand!*

Giving bad news
I'm afraid (that) the manager is in a meeting right now.
I'm sorry, but she's on another line.
Unfortunately, he's out of the office today.

Sounding confident
I'll make sure he emails you today.

3 Match the sentences on the left with the appropriate responses.

1 ☐ Thank you.
2 ☐ I'm afraid he's not in.
3 ☐ May I help you?
4 ☐ I'll make sure he gets the message right away.
5 ☐ Unfortunately, I got cut off.
6 ☐ Could I leave him a message?
7 ☐ My name is Mauricio Velasquez.
8 ☐ I'm sorry. Could you spell that, please?

a Thank you. I really appreciate it.
b Yes, certainly. I'll just get a pen.
c You're welcome.
d Yes, I have a question about your price list.
e That's OK. I'll call back later.
f Yes, it's P–F–A– double-F.
g Oh, I'm terribly sorry about that. Let me put you through again.
h I'm sorry. I didn't quite catch that.

4 Complete the sentences with the correct forms of the phrasal verbs in the box.

> cut off · get back to · get through · look up · put through · speak up

1 I'll .... the address in our directory for you.
2 This is a terrible line. You'll have to .... a bit.
3 There is something wrong with his extension. I tried it and was ....
4 I keep calling, but I can't .... to the help desk.
5 I'm sorry, but Ms. Allen is in a meeting right now. I've asked her to .... you as soon as she's free.
6 When I called the hotel, the operator .... me .... to the general manager's office.

5 Use the diagram to create a conversation you might need to have on the phone at work. Then practice your telephone call with a partner.

A Answer the phone.

B Say who you are and ask to speak to X. (It's urgent.)

A X is in a meeting. Message?

B Ask when X will be finished with the meeting.

A Respond. Message?

B Give your contact details and leave a message.

A Confirm caller's contact details and message.

B Confirm or correct contact details and message.

A Thank the caller and say goodbye.

6 Complete the steps in a telephone call by giving each list of telephoning phrases a heading.

Assuring the caller · Giving action points · Identifying yourself · Saying why you're calling ·
Showing attention · Showing follow-up · Summarizing · Understanding the caller ·
Wrapping up with the customer

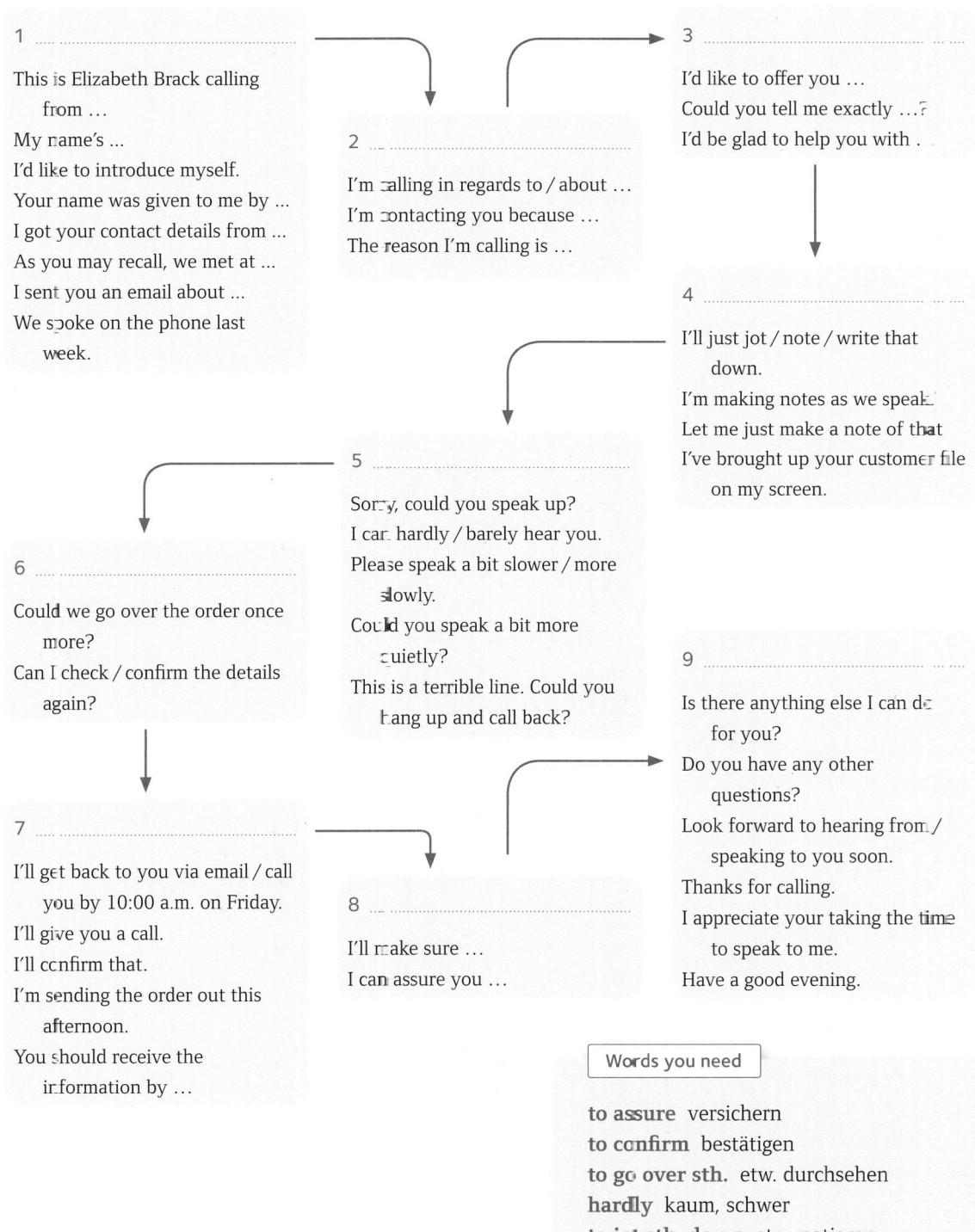

1 ....

This is Elizabeth Brack calling
   from …
My name's …
I'd like to introduce myself.
Your name was given to me by …
I got your contact details from …
As you may recall, we met at …
I sent you an email about …
We spoke on the phone last
   week.

2 ....

I'm calling in regards to / about …
I'm contacting you because …
The reason I'm calling is …

3 ....

I'd like to offer you …
Could you tell me exactly …?
I'd be glad to help you with .

4 ....

I'll just jot / note / write that
   down.
I'm making notes as we speak.
Let me just make a note of that
I've brought up your customer file
   on my screen.

5 ....

Sorry, could you speak up?
I can hardly / barely hear you.
Please speak a bit slower / more
   slowly.
Could you speak a bit more
   quietly?
This is a terrible line. Could you
   hang up and call back?

6 ....

Could we go over the order once
   more?
Can I check / confirm the details
   again?

7 ....

I'll get back to you via email / call
   you by 10:00 a.m. on Friday.
I'll give you a call.
I'll confirm that.
I'm sending the order out this
   afternoon.
You should receive the
   information by …

8 ....

I'll make sure …
I can assure you …

9 ....

Is there anything else I can do
   for you?
Do you have any other
   questions?
Look forward to hearing from /
   speaking to you soon.
Thanks for calling.
I appreciate your taking the time
   to speak to me.
Have a good evening.

> **Words you need**
>
> **to assure** versichern
> **to confirm** bestätigen
> **to go over sth.** etw. durchsehen
> **hardly** kaum, schwer
> **to jot sth. down** etw. notieren

7 Match the sentence halves to form sentences you would say during a telephone call.

1 ▢ I'll give you a call …
2 ▢ Look forward to …
3 ▢ Could you tell me …
4 ▢ I'm sending it overnight mail, …
5 ▢ I'm just jotting …
6 ▢ Thanks so much …
7 ▢ Let's go over it again …
8 ▢ Is there anything else …

a   your name, please?
b   by 5:00 today.
c   seeing you in the meeting.
d   for taking the time to call us.
e   that down.
f   I can help you with today?
g   to be sure of the details.
h   so you should receive it by
     twelve noon tomorrow.

*Stay away from
Have a nice day!
It's overused
and meaningless
nowadays. Try
other phrases like
Have a nice weekend /
evening or Enjoy
the nice weather
in Los Angeles!*

👥 Read the sentence halves in the left-hand column to a partner, and ask him/her to think of another way to complete each sentence.

8 Setting up appointments or meetings requires professional language. Complete the headings with the words in the box.

> Agreeing · Apologizing · Asking · Confirming · Deciding · Suggesting

1 ....
for an appointment or meeting
Could we schedule / set up / fix an appointment?
Are you available / free on Monday?
Does next Thursday suit you?
How about 2:00 p.m. on Tuesday?

2 ....
on a time
Just let me check my calendar / schedule.
Yes, Tuesday is fine with me.
Sounds good. Tuesday at 2:00 p.m., then.

3 ....
a new time
I'm sorry, but I'm tied up on Wednesday.
How about Tuesday morning instead?
Actually, Thursday morning would work better for me.

4 ....
where to meet
Shall I come to your office, or would you
   like to meet here?
Let's meet in the conference room.

5 ....
the appointment or meeting
We'll see each other next Thursday at 11:00
   a.m. at your office.
I'll pencil in Wednesday, but I need to check
   something with my colleague.
Could you confirm the details in an email?
Here's my cell phone number in case you need
   to reach me.
I look forward to seeing you.

6 ....
and suggesting alternatives
Sorry, I can't make the meeting on Tuesday.
Something has come up.
Unfortunately, I can't come / attend.
Could we postpone the meeting until …?
Could we reschedule the meeting to …?
How / What about …?

┌─ **Words you need** ─────────────────────────┐
to come up dazwischen kommen
to not make (a meeting) es nicht (zu einem Meeting)
     schaffen
to pencil in mit Bleistift eintragen, vorläufig vormerken
to reach s.o. jmd. erreichen
to suit passen
└──┘

9 Match the questions with the responses.

1. ☐ Can we fix a meeting for next Tuesday at 9:00 a.m.?
2. ☐ Is Friday the 18th convenient for you?
3. ☐ Could we set up an appointment for Thursday afternoon?
4. ☐ Are you free next Monday for a meeting?
5. ☐ How about 1:00 p.m. in my office?

a. Monday? Yes, that's fine with me.
b. 1:00 is fine with me, but I'd prefer to meet in my office, if that's OK.
c. Sorry, I'm tied up that morning. How about 1:30 instead?
d. I'm off for a long weekend on that date. Can I call you when I get back?
e. Yes, that sounds good. Is two o'clock OK?

Practice reading the questions and answers with a partner. Then try the questions and answers again using different times and dates.

> When you can't set up a meeting because you're busy, use expressions like *I'm tied up / I'm not available* not *I'm too busy! / I have no time! / I can't*. Soften refusals with *I'm afraid* or *unfortunately*.
> *I'm afraid I'm not available then.*
> *Unfortunately, I'm tied up on Thursday.*
>
> Try to avoid saying *That's not possible* or *That's impossible*. This is sometimes said in English, but not nearly as much as it is in German, and it may sound impolite.

10 Complete the phone dialogue. In some cases, more than one answer may be used.

Carol: Carol Warner .... .¹

Hannah: Hi Carol. This is Hannah from Creative Concepts. How are you? How's the

.... ² in Houston?

Carol: Oh, hello Hannah. Good to hear from you. I'm fine. It's still a bit warm here. Anyway, what

.... ³ I do for you today?

Hannah: Could we .... ⁴ a meeting for next week? .... ⁵ about Thursday at 10:00 a.m.?

Carol: Sorry, I'm a bit .... ⁶ on Thursday. Could we meet Wednesday at 2:00 p.m. instead?

Hannah: Yes, I'm .... ⁷ then. Where would be the best place to meet?

Carol: Well, I'll .... ⁸ the conference room. Let me .... ⁹ that with you by 5:00 p.m. today.

Hannah: Sounds good. Could you email me the confirmation? I'll be difficult to .... ¹⁰ by phone the rest of the day.

Carol: Sure, no problem.

Hannah: Well, look forward to seeing you at the meeting. Bye.

Carol: Likewise! See you then. Goodbye.

🔊 13 Listen to check your answers Then practice the phone call with a partner.

11 Practice this phone call to arrange a meeting with a partner. Then switch roles and try it again, this time to set up a video-conference.

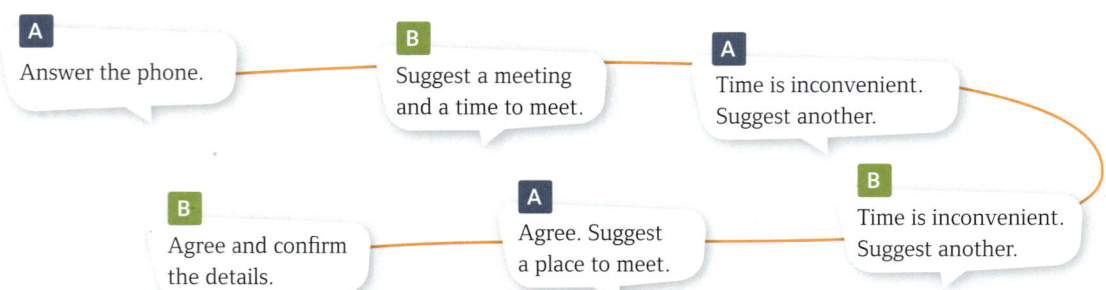

12 Check the following vocabulary for making arrangements. In each line, cross out one word that doesn't mean the same as the other words.

1 fix … arrange … set up … make … schedule (a meeting)
2 convenient … important … suitable … good (date and time)
3 comfortable … available … free (for a meeting or an appointment)
4 (can) make … attend … come to … arrange (a meeting)
5 postpone … move … cancel … delay (a meeting date and time)

Did you know?

In the US the term *cell phone* is used, while *mobile phone* is the international term outside the US.

13 ◁14 Listen to the voicemail message and read the written message. Circle the words you heard in the message.

Phone Note	
Message to: *Jon Marshal*	From: *Barbara Kennedy*
Date: *January 12*	Time: *4:23*

Message: *Regarding your appointment next week, something has gone down / come up[1]. She's afraid she can't make / can't meet[2] it on Monday. She'll be tried to / tied up[3] all day. Could you postpone / present[4] the meeting to Tuesday at 10:00 a.m.? Please let her know if that's convenient / comfortable[5] for you. Call or email her.*

✂

Phone Note

Message to:

14

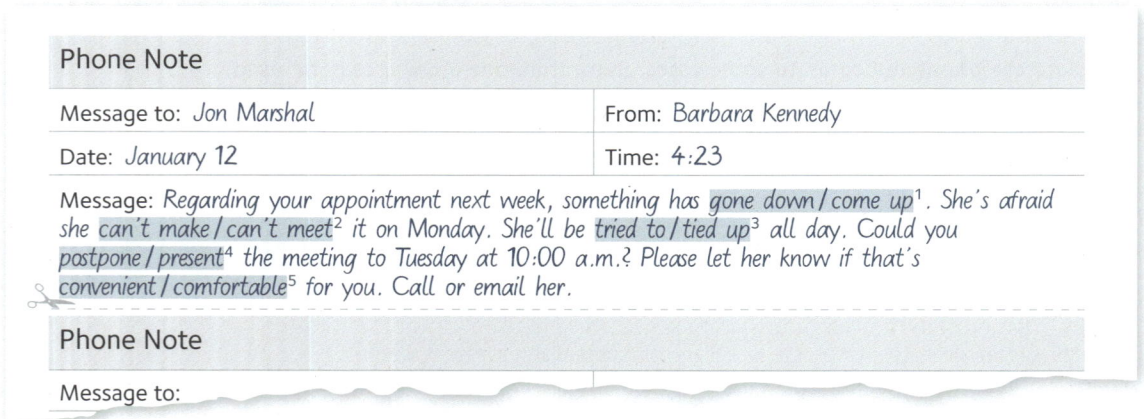

Simulation

👥 **Think of a type of meeting you often attend at work. Call a partner and apologize, explaining that you can't come to the meeting. Try to arrange another time to meet.**

Use the form on the right to prepare yourself. Use basic telephoning language and phrases for making arrangements and rescheduling meetings.

Identify yourself and say why you're calling:
....

Explain that you can't come to the meeting:
....

Apologize and suggest an alternative:
....

Confirm the date and time:
....

Customer Care Professionals

Home | **Customer Care Trends** | **Professional Events** | **Tips and Training** | **Contacts**

Home | **Tips and Training** | Improving English Language Skills

Building Confidence on the Phone

Dealing with phone calls in English can really be a test of nerves. You see the number on your phone coming in from the US – and panic can start to set in. Your first instinct is to transfer the call to your co-worker who speaks better English than you do.

How can we build our confidence on the phone in English? Isn't there anything we can do
5 to calm our nerves during English phone calls? Of course, we need to know the right professional language to use, but that's not all. Consider these tips from experts:

- Be prepared at any time for English calls from your customers. Keep your telephoning English language charts handy for these phone calls. Be ready to bring up a customer file on your computer any time the customer could call. Have your notepad ready to take
10   notes.

- Speak slowly. Don't be in a hurry! Take a moment to think about what you'd like to say. This can also prompt the caller to have a relaxed manner with you on the phone.

- Use words or phrases that give a confident feeling, such as "I'm sure we can ..." or "I'm confident we can ..." On the other hand, if you can't give the customer an answer,
15   then say, "I'll check on that and get back to you." Never say "I don't know" or "It might be possible." This causes a lot of uncertainty for the customer.

- Vary your voice to show your enthusiasm. A monotone voice gives the customer the idea that you are just plain bored with your job.

- Finally, listen and answer honestly and naturally, not just from a memorized script or
20   pitch. This establishes a base for building rapport with customers.

Your confidence can be felt on the phone, even though customers can't see you. This will also boost your confidence for further communication with the customer, either face-to-face, during a video-conference, or even via email.

Building confidence on the phone is a step-by-step
25 process. With each call, you will feel more at ease with your English-language skills and how you deal with customers. This means a positive working relationship for you and the customer!

Words you need
to boost fördern, steigern
to establish sth. etw. schaffen, aufbauen
handy griffbereit
memorized auswendig gelernt
pitch Verkaufstechnik
to prompt anregen, der Anlass für etw. sein

Over to you

- Do you agree with the tips in the article? Have you tried any of the suggestions? Does it seem to help with your nervousness?
- Can you add any other tips that have worked for you?

Unit 4 . Managing Customers on the Phone | 37

5 Call Center Success

In this unit you will …
- use basic call center and customer-focused language
- take an order
- ask for clarification, explain, and check comprehension
- make suggestions

With a partner, discuss this recent survey about call centers for retail industries in the US. Which percentages do you think are correct? Why? Check the key on page 70 to see the actual answers. Were there any surprises?

1 **12% 24% 42%** of calls were rated unsatisfactory.
2 Agents were rude in **11% 21% 31%** of calls.
3 **9% 16% 25%** of calls took more than three rings to answer.
4 In **7% 10% 14%** of calls, agents didn't have enough knowledge to handle the call.
5 In **32% 46% 62%** of calls, agents didn't spend enough time trying to understand the caller's actual needs.

Would a survey in your country have similar results? Why or why not? How could call centers improve their customer ratings?

1 ◁15 Listen to the two call center conversations and complete the table.

	Call 1	Call 2
Customer		
Customer is interested in		
Follow-up		

Can and could
Use *can* when offering to do something for the customer.
Can I help you?
Use *could* when asking the customer to do something.
Could you give me your mailing address?

2 ♪15 Listen again to the phone calls. Complete these sentences from the dialogues.

1 .... that you need some assistance.

2 .... type this in … one moment …

3 As .... it, the problem starts when you enter the password?

4 .... the service technicians' schedule and ....

5 One moment, let me just .... your customer file on my screen.

6 .... your order as urgent.

7 .... for your order.

3 Write the phrases in the box next to the appropriate tip for using customer-focused language.

And how long have you had this problem? · Can I help you with anything else? ·
Can I assist you with anything else today? · Could you tell me …? · Does that sound all right? ·
How can I help you? · I'll call you back in half an hour. · I'll call you when … to make sure
everything went well. · I'll flag your order as urgent. · It seems that you need some assistance?
OK, let me repeat that. · So, as I understand it … Is that right? · Thank you for your order. ·
What can I do for you? · Yes, I can understand how important it is.

1 **Signal a friendly, ready-to-help attitude with your tone and voice.**

2 **Show that you are listening carefully.**

3 **Ask for more information, show understanding, and check satisfaction.**

4 **Make promises and keep them, and show follow-up and follow-through.**

5 **Ask if the customer needs anything more, and thank the customer.**

Can you add any other tips? Discuss which tips you could improve upon with a partner.

4 Match the sentence halves to make complete sentences.

1	How can I …	a	all right?
2	I will make sure …	b	of this right away.
3	I hope this is …	c	help you?
4	Could you give me …	d	repeat that.
5	Is there anything else …	e	you receive the information this afternoon.
6	I'll take care …	f	I can assist you with today?
7	Let me just …	g	your account number, please?

5 ◁ 16 Listen to the telephone call and complete the dialogue with the words you hear.

Agent: Good morning. Ace Town Beverages Helpline. 1

Customer: Yes, please. I need to place an order for ten more cases of my standard house wine.

Agent: It sounds like you have ordered from us before. 2

Customer: Of course, here it is … uh … 55008-22.

Agent: Ah yes, Mr. Green from Suavo Restaurant. 3
So, that's Breitestrasse …

Customer: No, that's our old address. We've just moved to Hauptstrasse 43. The zip code is still 45221.

Agent: 4
That's Hauptstrasse 43, zip code 45221.

Customer: 5

Agent: OK, I've updated our database. Let me just type in the order … OK …

Customer: Look, I'm really in a bind. Could you do a rush order so that we get it by tomorrow morning?

Agent: Sure, that's no problem. We can dispatch today for overnight delivery. OK, Mr. Green,

.... 6 You'd like your standard order of house wine.
And we'll rush the order so it arrives around 10:00 a.m.

Customer: Yes, that's correct. Thanks for being so helpful.

Agent: 7

 Now practice the dialogue with a partner.

Words you need

to be in a bind in der Klemme stecken
database Datenbank
to dispatch abschicken
to place (an order) (eine Bestellung)
  aufgeben
to rush beschleunigen, antreiben
rush order Eilauftrag
zip code (US), postcode (UK) Postleitzahl

6 🔊 17 Listen to the international spelling system (NATO phonetic alphabet). Then practice saying the alphabet.

Alfa	Echo	India	Mike	Quebec	Uniform	Yankee
Bravo	Foxtrot	Juliet	November	Romeo	Victor	Zulu
Charlie	Golf	Kilo	Oscar	Sierra	Whiskey	
Delta	Hotel	Lima	Papa	Tango	X-ray	

Now spell your name and street name for your partner using the alphabet. Write down your partner's name and street name as they're spelled out. Then compare notes. Have you spelled everything correctly?

7 Look at the following dialogue. How would you improve the agent's language to make it more customer-focused?

Customer: Hello? This is John Norman speaking.
Agent: Hello, Mr. Norman. Need some help today? ¹
Customer: I'd like to order accounting software.
Agent: Accounting software. Which one? ²
Customer: Um, the latest accounting software package you have listed on your website.
Agent: Have you ordered stuff from us before? ³
Customer: Yes, a few times.
Agent: I need your customer number, then. ⁴
Customer: OK, let me look it up … Here it is. It's 5853579.
Agent: OK, how many of the software packages do you want? ⁵
Customer: I'd like five, please.
Agent: Good. Now I need your address. ⁶
Customer: 234 Harris Street, Los Angeles, California. And the zip code is 90063.
Agent: Fine. I've got that. Anything else? ⁷
Customer: Well, when will I receive it?
Agent: Maybe sometime next week. I've got another call coming in, so I need to go now! ⁸

Write customer-focused sentences here to replace sentences 1–8 in the dialogue.

1
2 ....
3 ....
4 ....
5 ....
6 ....
7 ....
8 ....

Practice the dialogue with a partner using your new customer-friendly phrases.

8 ◁18 **Listen to the telephone conversation and complete the notes.**

Product ....

Problem ....

....

Action taken ....

....

Words you need

to clarify
(näher) erläutern
free of charge
kostenlos
system requirement
Systemanforderung

Listen again and tick the sentences you hear.

1 ▢ So, what exactly is the problem?
2 ▢ Could you explain the problem in more detail?
3 ▢ Could you explain what you've done so far?
4 ▢ That means you need to have …
5 ▢ In other words, you need to have …
6 ▢ Do you follow me?

7 ▢ Do you understand?
8 ▢ Do you see that?
9 ▢ Is that clear?
10 ▢ Let me just talk you through the steps.
11 ▢ This is what I'm going to do.
12 ▢ By the way, have you registered with us?

9 **Match a heading to each phrase used in a call center.**

A Asking for clarification   **B** Explaining   **C** Checking comprehension

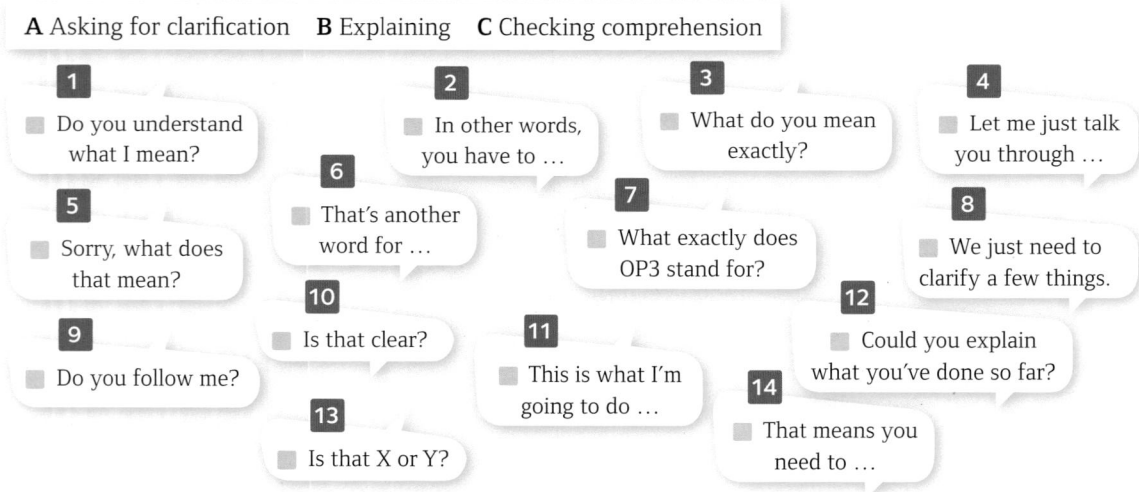

1
▢ Do you understand what I mean?

2
▢ In other words, you have to …

3
▢ What do you mean exactly?

4
▢ Let me just talk you through …

5
▢ Sorry, what does that mean?

6
▢ That's another word for …

7
▢ What exactly does OP3 stand for?

8
▢ We just need to clarify a few things.

9
▢ Do you follow me?

10
▢ Is that clear?

11
▢ This is what I'm going to do …

12
▢ Could you explain what you've done so far?

13
▢ Is that X or Y?

14
▢ That means you need to …

10 **Choose suitable words to complete the call center phrases.**

1 We just need to .... a few things.

2 Do you .... me so far?

3 Could you .... what you've done so far?

4 That .... you need to install some software.

5 What does OP3 .... for?

6 This is .... I'm going to do.

7 Let me just .... you through the steps.

👥 **With a partner, discuss the steps to use a service or product that your company sells.**

11 ◁ 19 Complete these extracts from a call center dialogue with language for making suggestions. Then listen to check your answers.

Customer: I'm having trouble with my cable TV and internet system. It turns on and seems to work, but I can't get any channels on the TV. Then the internet icon on my computer says it's connected, but there's still no access.

Agent: Oh, I'm so sorry to hear about that. OK, I'm going to need to ask you some questions.

.... ¹ unplugging the cables and reconnecting them?

Customer: Yes, but it still doesn't seem to work.

Agent: .... ² turning the main system box for the TV and internet on and off?

Customer: I've tried that as well. I've also pushed every button on the remote control to at least get something moving on the TV.

Agent: Well, it sounds like we really need to send out a technician. In the meantime,

.... ³ not using the remote control for the TV. When would be a convenient time to set up an appointment?

Customer: Is there any way I can watch any TV until then?

Agent: .... ⁴ switch off the cable box and just watch the local channels?

Customer: Thanks very much. I'll do that!

Words you need
channel Sender
to suggest vorschlagen
to unplug entfernen, ausstöpseln

Practice the conversation with a partner.

Phrases to use

Why don't you …?

Have you tried …?

Should / Could we try …?

Making suggestions

How about …?

I'd recommend / suggest …

Why not …?

You could try …

12 Think of two customer care problems that often occur at work. How might you solve them? Write sentences using suggestion language to present ideas for solving the problems.

1 ....

....

2 ....

....

3 ....

....

4 ....

....

13 Choose the best response in these call center situations.

1

Can't you give me a better price for our first order?

a Sorry, I can't do that.

b Let me check with the manager and call you back in a few minutes.

c It might be possible.

2

Can you quote me a price?

a The price is a fair one.

b They cost about 40 cents each.

c Our price is better than our competitors' prices.

3

We are thinking of signing up for your service.

a Then why don't you take advantage of our introductory offer?

b Call us back when you've decided.

c I told you our prices yesterday.

4

Can you do a rush order for me?

a I'll try.

b Of course. This will go out by the end of the day.

c We can't process orders in a hurry, sorry.

5

I'd like to order five cases, please.

a OK, that's five cases.

b Are you sure you only want five?

c We have a special offer today: you get one case free when you order six.

6

When can the order be dispatched?

a Today, sir, by overnight delivery.

b Maybe this evening.

c Our deliveries today are all backed up.

> **Words you need**
>
> **to back up** stauen
> **to quote** anbieten
> **to take advantage of** (eine Gelegenheit) nutzen

> When you can't help a customer, say We are unable to offer / provide that, not We can't offer / provide that. Then try to suggest an alternative.

14

Simulation

👥 **With a partner, discuss how you deal with customer questions or inquiries in your company.**

Use the basic call center and customer-focused language you've learned. Consider how you might ask for clarification, explain, check comprehension, or make suggestions.

Types of customer questions or inquiries:

1 ....
2 ....
3 ....
4 ....

Language needed for questions and inquiries:

1 ....
2 ....
3 ....
4 ....

Call Center Trends

The call center business is constantly evolving to meet changes in the
global business environment. These changes include customer use of web,
telephone, email, and social media, especially Facebook and Twitter,
to communicate about products and services. Customers now enjoy many
5 more ways to communicate, and the challenge for call centers today is to
meet a broader range of demands while using more dynamic technology.

Experts have identified the following customer support trends in this
changing business environment.

Emotion Detection

10 Emotion detection is a buzz phrase to describe and measure how callers feel. It is based on signals like
how loud customers are talking, their tone and pitch, and how fast they speak. We are seeing more
specialized technology for detecting the emotions of the customer. Some call centers prioritize callers or
hold based on their level of emotion. Emotion detection technology has great potential to turn frustrated
and angry customers into happy ones.

15 ### Scheduled Call-Backs

Nothing is more frustrating to a caller than having to wait on hold. In response, some companies call
customers back instead of making them wait on hold. This helps ease the frustration and meet the
service demands of the customer.

Organizing Call Center Data

20 Technology is giving call centers access to more data than ever before. However, the volume of
information is often simply stored data that's not put to good use. Managers are finding ways to organize
and use this data. This will help make call center operations more helpful to customers and more
profitable for businesses.

Agent Attrition

25 Call center agents normally experience a lot of stress. They deal with rude
customers, are constantly monitored, and are underpaid. Not surprisingly,
call centers have the highest employee turnover rate of any industry.
Reducing agent attrition, or keeping agents in their jobs, allows call centers
to spend less money on training new agents. This is usually one of their
30 biggest expenses. Experts expect to see more focus on allowing agents to
work from home, providing updated knowledge-based training, and creating
systems with scheduled call-backs. These initiatives could make an agent's
life easier and less stressful. This is key to keeping agents happy and
satisfied in their jobs.

Words you need
attrition Verschleiß, Verlust
buzz phrase Schlagwort
constantly ständig
to detect erfassen, erkennen
to measure messen, abschätzen
pitch Tonhöhe
turnover Fluktuation
underpaid unterbezahlt

Over to you

· What trends and changes have you noticed in the customer care business?
  Which do you think is most important and why?
· What are the current trends being talked about in your company?
· What training is offered in your company to keep call center employees up to date?

In this unit you will …

- identify formal and informal writing styles
- use writing styles correctly
- write effective business communications
- deal with the social media writing style

6 Delivering Customer Care through Writing

Answer the following questions about email styles. Then compare answers with a partner.

1 What do you think the relationships between the people in the photos are? Would they write to one another in a formal or an informal style?
2 Who do you write to in a formal style?
3 Who do you write to in an informal style?
4 How do these styles differ from one another? Write down any examples you can think of.
5 If a customer or client writes to you in an informal style, in which style should you respond?

1 Look at these excerpts from emails. Mark each message as formal (F) or informal (I). How can you tell?

A

Hi Oliver,

We're having a going-away party for our colleague, Klaus Braun, next Friday at 2:00 p.m. We're meeting up in the executive conference room on the 10th floor.
I know you worked with him for many years, so it'd be great if you could join us.

Please tell me if you can come. Looking forward to seeing you at the party.

Best wishes,
Jörg

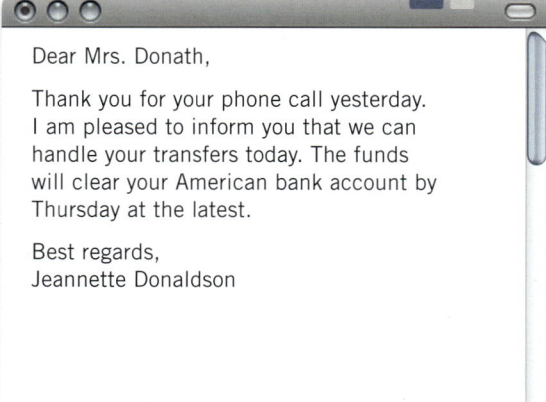

B

Dear Mrs. Donath,

Thank you for your phone call yesterday. I am pleased to inform you that we can handle your transfers today. The funds will clear your American bank account by Thursday at the latest.

Best regards,
Jeannette Donaldson

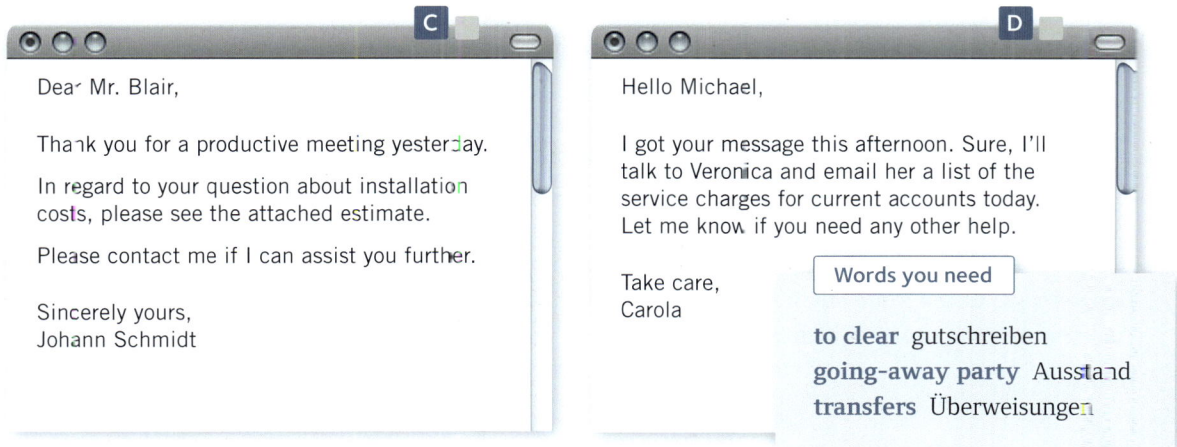

C

Dear Mr. Blair,

Thank you for a productive meeting yesterday.

In regard to your question about installation costs, please see the attached estimate.

Please contact me if I can assist you further.

Sincerely yours,
Johann Schmidt

D

Hello Michael,

I got your message this afternoon. Sure, I'll talk to Veronica and email her a list of the service charges for current accounts today. Let me know if you need any other help.

Take care,
Carola

Words you need

to clear gutschreiben
going-away party Ausstand
transfers Überweisungen

2   With a partner, complete the text about the style differences you can see in the emails in Exercise 1.

A   In very formal writing the verbs are in the .... ¹ form, not contracted as in a more

informal style. For example, we say *I am pleased* in a formal way, and .... ² *glad*
informally.

B   A full subject and verb is always used in .... ³ style. The .... ⁴
can sometimes be dropped and only the verb used in informal writing. We can say *I am looking forward* in

a .... ⁵ way or *Looking forward* in an informal style.

C   We use higher-level words and phrases for the .... ⁶ style. For example, in formal

writing we would use *assist* instead of the informal word .... ⁷ We can write *Please*

contact me if I can assist you further in a formal way, or .... ⁸ informally.

Phrases to use

When you don't know the name: Formal

· Dear Sir or Madam,
· Ladies and Gentlemen,
· To Whom It May Concern:
· Sincerely (yours),
· Yours faithfully,

When you don't know the name: Informal

· Hello,
· (Kind) Regards,
· Best wishes,

When you know the name but don't know the person well: Formal

· Dear Mr./Ms./Mrs. Smith,
· Dear Mr. and Mrs. Smith,
· Dear Ms. Black and Mr. Smith,
· Sincerely (yours),
· Yours faithfully,

Salutations and closings

When you know the name but don't know the person well: Informal

· Dear / Hello Mr./Ms.,
· Mrs. Smith,
· Dear / Hello Mr. and Mrs. Smith,
· Dear / Hello Ms. Black and Mr. Smith,
· Best wishes,
· All the best,

When you know the person / people well: Informal

Dear / Hello / Hi John,
Hi Paul and Mary,
Best (wishes),
All the best,
Take care,

When you know the person / people well: Formal

· Dear John,
· Dear Paul and Mary,
· Sincerely (yours),
· (Kind) Regards,
· Best wishes,

3 Two versions of the same email – one formal and one informal – have been mixed up. Put them back in order. Which is formal and which informal?

Dear Mr. Vogt,

1 ▢
2 ▢
3 ▢
4 ▢

Hi Manfred,

1 ▢
2 ▢
3 ▢
4 ▢

Unlike in German, the first word in letters and emails always starts with a capital letter.

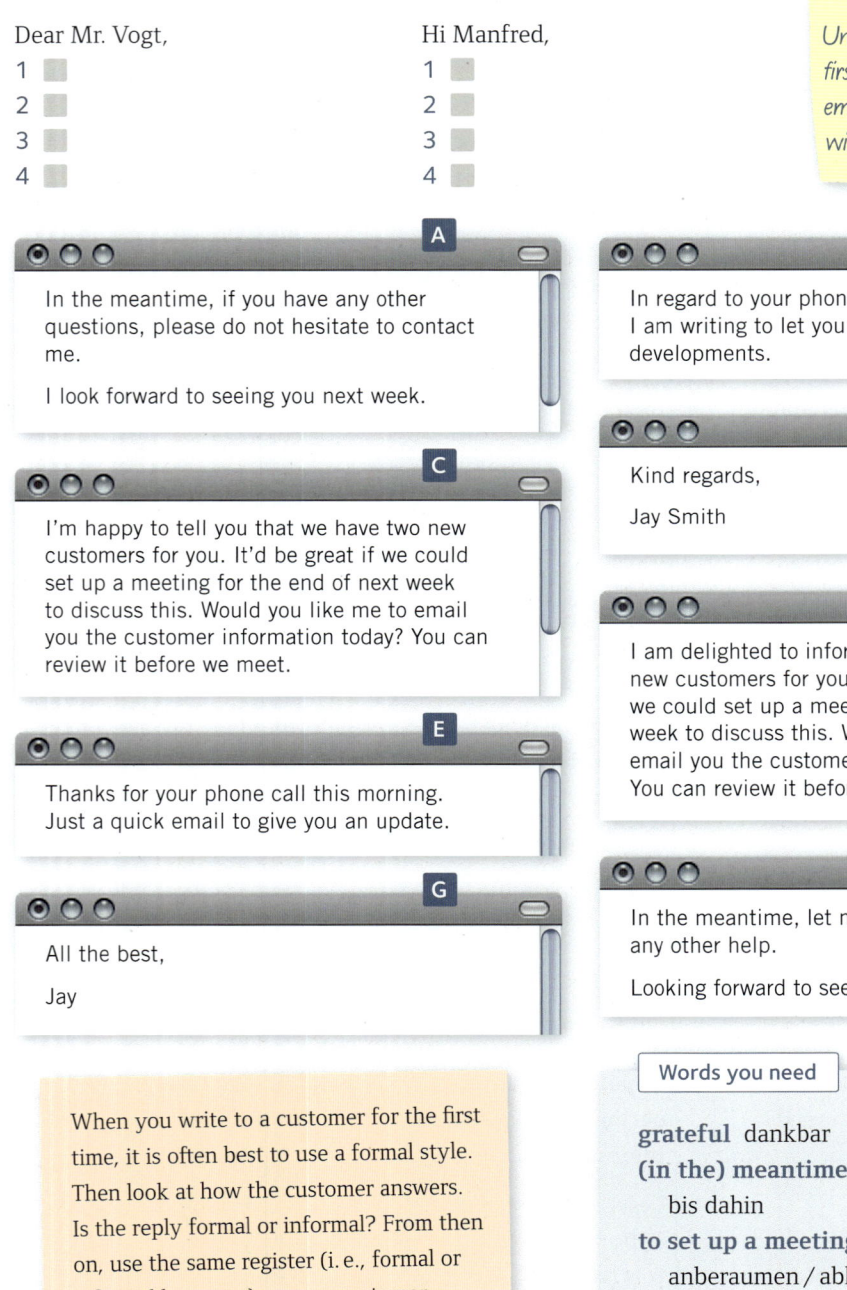

A
In the meantime, if you have any other questions, please do not hesitate to contact me.

I look forward to seeing you next week.

B
In regard to your phone call this morning, I am writing to let you know about the latest developments.

C
I'm happy to tell you that we have two new customers for you. It'd be great if we could set up a meeting for the end of next week to discuss this. Would you like me to email you the customer information today? You can review it before we meet.

D
Kind regards,

Jay Smith

E
Thanks for your phone call this morning. Just a quick email to give you an update.

F
I am delighted to inform you that we have two new customers for you. I would be grateful if we could set up a meeting for the end of next week to discuss this. Would you like me to email you the customer information today? You can review it before we meet.

G
All the best,

Jay

H
In the meantime, let me know if you need any other help.

Looking forward to seeing you next week.

When you write to a customer for the first time, it is often best to use a formal style. Then look at how the customer answers. Is the reply formal or informal? From then on, use the same register (i. e., formal or informal language) as your customer.

Words you need

grateful dankbar
(in the) meantime in der Zwischenzeit, bis dahin
to set up a meeting ein Meeting anberaumen / abhalten

4 The box on page 47 and two emails in Exercise 3 show formal and informal styles of letter writing. Complete the box with a word or phrase in the correct style.

	Formal	Informal
Salutation	Dear Mr. Vogt,	.... [1] Manfred,
Body Text	In .... [2] to your phone call, I am .... to .... [4] you … If you have any .... [6] questions, do not hesitate to contact me.	.... [3] for your phone call. I'm .... to .... [5] you … Let .... [7] if you need any other help.
Closing	.... [8] regards,	.... [9] the best,

Can you add any more formal or informal language from the emails in Exercise 1 or that you've come across in your personal or professional life? For more ideas, review the list of useful phrases on page 76.

These examples of formal and informal style are common in business writing. However, levels of formality or informality often depend on individual company cultures. The styles, either completely formal or informal, or even mixed, can be dictated by company policies.

5 Circle the best words or phrases to complete a formal message to a new customer.

Hi / Dear[1] Mr. Kaufmann,

I was pleased / I was glad[2] to meet you recently at the BankExpo Trade Fair. **I'm happy / I am delighted**[3] to be able to **assist / help**[4] you in finding a suitable IT communication system for your bank. As you requested, **I have attached / I've attached**[5] our latest catalogue with details and prices.

It would be great / I would be grateful[6] if we could meet soon. **I'll call / will call**[7] you on Thursday so we can arrange a convenient date and time.

If you have any further questions, please do not hesitate to contact me / Let me know if you have any other questions.[8]

I am looking forward / Looking forward[9] to having you as a new customer.

Take care / Sincerely yours,[10]

George Brown

Sales Manager

6 Mr. Kaufmann answers George Brown's email. Complete the reply with suitable words and phrases from the list in an informal style. Note that there are more words and phrases than you need.

> Dear · glad · Hi · I am · I am looking · I'll let you know · I'm · I will inform you · I would like to set up · Let's set up · Looking · pleased · regards · wishes

....¹ George,

Thanks a lot for your message. I was also very ....² to have the opportunity to meet you at the trade fair.

....³ very interested in your IT communication system products and services.

....⁴ a meeting for next week. Could you call me on Thursday around 11:00?

In the meantime, ...⁵ if I've got any other questions.

....⁶ forward to hearing from you again.

Best ....⁷,

Helmut

Simulation

7

Choose one formal and one informal email to write from the list.

Exchange emails with a partner. Is there anything you would change about your partner's email? As a class, write a collection of useful phrases on the board.

1 Write an email to a new customer you've just met. Ask for his/her mailing address and phone numbers.
2 Write an email to a colleague you don't know. Ask him/her to send you something related to your work.
3 Write a message to a colleague. Ask him/her to meet up with you next week for lunch at the employee cafeteria.
4 Write an email to a colleague you know well. Ask him/her if he/she has time for a quick meeting tomorrow. Tell him/her what you'd like to discuss.

---

8 This follow-up email to a new customer is written in an informal style. With a partner, replace or edit the highlighted words or phrases to be more suitable for a new customer.

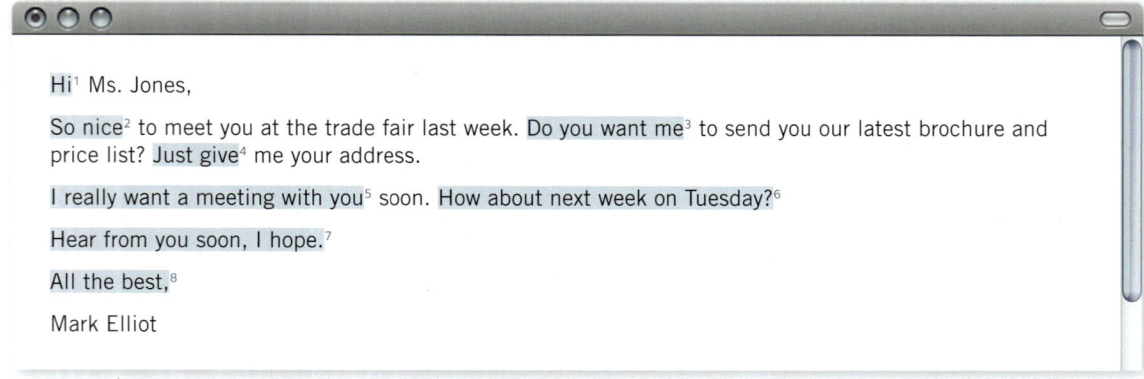

Hi¹ Ms. Jones,

So nice² to meet you at the trade fair last week. Do you want me³ to send you our latest brochure and price list? Just give⁴ me your address.

I really want a meeting with you⁵ soon. How about next week on Tuesday?⁶

Hear from you soon, I hope.⁷

All the best,⁸

Mark Elliot

Enclosures and attachments

Make sure you review your documents carefully before sending them to the customer. Take an extra moment to check the enclosures or attachments before you close the envelope or hit the send button!

Please note that *to enclose* and *enclosure* are used only for sending documents by regular mail or post.
To attach and *attachment* are used in emails only. The verb *to include* can be used for faxes.

Phrases to use

Formal

· Please find enclosed / attached …
· In the enclosed, …
· I have attached …
· As you will see in the enclosed / attached …

Enclosures and attachments

Informal

· I'm sending you … as an attachment.
· I've attached … as a PDF document.
· The … you requested is attached.
· Here's the … you asked for.

9 Use the language you've learned in this unit so far and the list of useful phrases on page 76 to write a customer-friendly reply to the email inquiry.

Hello,

I have just visited your relocation services website. I will soon be moving to Berlin, so I am looking for an agency to help me find an apartment. Can you also recommend a place to lease a car for my business?

I was not able to find any information about your prices on your website, so could you please email me the current price list? Also, I will be in Berlin at the end of the month. Could we perhaps set up a meeting? My cell phone number is 0188 59773.

Thank you for your assistance. I look forward to hearing from you and hope to meet you soon.

Regards,

Joan White

White Associates

jwhite@whiteassociates.com

Exchange emails with a partner. Have you both used the correct level of formality consistently? Give your partner tips for improving his/her email.

10 With a partner, write out the abbreviations and acronyms in full. Can you think of any others?

1	asap	6	2moro	
2	FYI	7	ur	
3	BTW	8	mgr	
4	RE	9	fwd	
5	mtg	10	pls	

11 ◁20 **Listen to the interview about the effect of textspeak on professional writing and mark the sentences true or false.**

		True	False
1	Dr. Vaught's studies show that textspeak has no effect on communication.	▨	▨
2	People who use textspeak are as careful about language as those who don't.	▨	▨
3	The radio host suggests that it's OK to write quick text messages or tweets as long as they follow the conventions for that type of communication.	▨	▨
4	Innovation in language is always negative.	▨	▨
5	Those who use textspeak tend to be less interested in writing properly.	▨	▨

Do you agree with Dr. Vaught's points? How much do you text or tweet in your customer contact?

> **Words you need**
>
> **to assume** vermuten
> **to conduct sth.**
>   etw. durchführen
> **to decipher** entschlüsseln
> **to discover** entdecken
>
> **established** bekannt, etabliert
> **evidence** Beweis, Beleg
> **to presume** annehmen
> **sloppy** nachlässig, schludrig
> **succinct** bündig, prägnant

As a general rule, PLZ (please) avoid textspeak (abbreviations and acronyms) in professional writing. You may be ROFLOL (rolling on the floor laughing out loud), but your reader may be left wondering WUWT (what's up with that).

12 **Rewrite these text or Twitter messages in full words and complete phrases.**

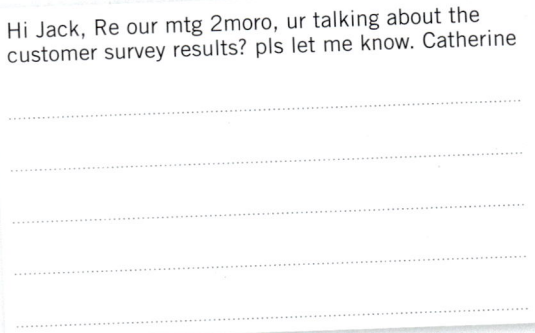

Hi Jack, Re our mtg 2moro, ur talking about the customer survey results? pls let me know. Catherine

Tweets

Jack Miller @JackMiller50 9 mins
Hi Catherine. Yes, will talk about the results. BTW, the mgr is happy with the feedback!

13 **Write these formal email messages as informal texts or tweets.**

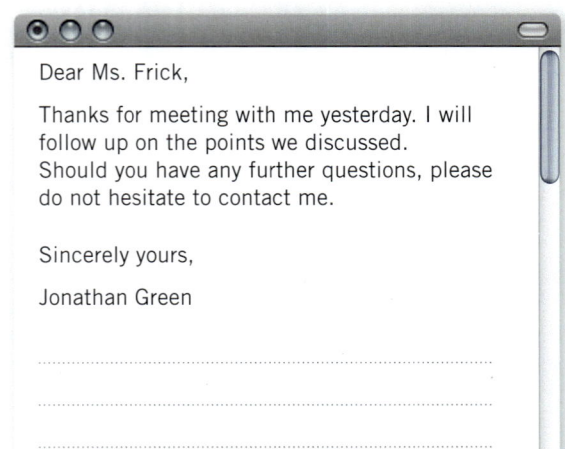

Dear Ms. Frick,

Thanks for meeting with me yesterday. I will follow up on the points we discussed. Should you have any further questions, please do not hesitate to contact me.

Sincerely yours,

Jonathan Green

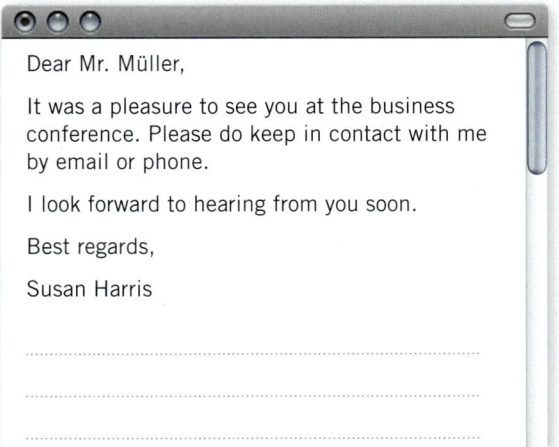

Dear Mr. Müller,

It was a pleasure to see you at the business conference. Please do keep in contact with me by email or phone.

I look forward to hearing from you soon.

Best regards,

Susan Harris

Customer Care Today

business magazine

High-Impact Emails to Customers

Recent studies published in business journals have suggested ways to increase the impact of emails to customers. The message needs to show solid action and
5 be relevant to the customer's needs.

So, what does that actually mean? It means that customer service needs to deliver a good concrete response that makes a positive impression. Customers
10 also need to see you are focusing entirely on them – their inquiries, problems, or complaints. They want to feel confident about your service after reading your email.

15 To create a high-impact email, begin with the following principles:

- Be courteous. Address customers professionally and politely in the correct style.
20 • Be clear. Let the customer know why you are writing and which issue you are dealing with.

- Be actionable and concise. Get to the
25 point in a polite way. State the situation and how you can handle it for the customer.

A great high-impact email does all of this and more. It also makes the customer
30 feel like the center of attention without being overbearing. Moreover, this kind of email helps the customer feel good about the brand and the company. When the sender cares about how the email
35 message comes across, the customer feels inspired to share the experience with friends and associates. High-impact emails do not need to be lengthy and complicated – just honest, direct, and
40 positive.

Words you need

associate Geschäftsfreund
to come across auf andere wirken
courteous höflich
to inspire anregen
overbearing überheblich
principle Grundlage, Richtlinie

Over to you

- Can you add any other important high-impact tips to the article?
- What do you expect in a professional email? How does an unprofessional email affect your motivation to help a colleague or customer?
- With a partner, discuss an unprofessional email you received and how you dealt with it in a professional manner.
- How could cultural differences have an impact on email communication? Share your experiences with a partner.

In this unit you will …
· discuss typical customer complaints
· solve problems in English
· respond to complaints
· explain policies
· consider the impact of social media on customer complaints

7 Handling Problems and Complaints

Look at this list of situations that customers complain about. Which three things annoy you the most as a customer?

Dealing with a complicated automated answering system

Being put on hold

Salespeople with poor knowledge of their products and services

Being transferred multiple times

Not enough staff to help customers

Not getting quick answers to emails

Receiving too much junk mail or advertising

Getting a busy signal

Getting complicated, unclear explanations

Unfriendly staff

Can you add anything else to the list?
Compare your answers with a partner's. How can companies deal with each type of complaint?

1 ◁)21 Listen to the customer service director talking to his staff about customer complaints, and mark in what order he says these words.

☐ a annoyed	☐ c condescending	☐ e mistake	☐ g resolve
☐ b apologize	☐ d fault	☐ f policy	☐ h shout

2   Complete the action checklist with words from Exercise 1.

Sample action checklist for customer complaints at the bank

☑ Listen carefully to the customer. This will help calm the ....[1] customer.

☑ Talking in a loud voice is never a solution. Don't ever ....[2] at the customer.

☑ Having an arrogant attitude is not customer care. We can't be ....[3] to the customer.

☑ We can't say it was the customer's ....[4]. We should talk about the problem in a neutral way, without blaming one side or the other.

☑ We need to admit we've made a ....[5] and then move on to finding a solution.

☑ The first actual step in dealing with the complaint is to ....[6] to the customer, no matter who caused the problem.

☑ We should try to look carefully at our company ....[7] to find any reasonable solution to solve the problem.

☑ We have to take care of and ....[8] problems and complaints with respect.

🗨 Do you agree with the tips? Can you add two other ideas to the checklist for handling complaints? Share your ideas with a partner.

3   ◁ 22 Three customers are making complaints. Listen and match the dialogues to the pictures. Then complete the table.

	Complaint	Response
Dialogue 1		
Dialogue 2		
Dialogue 3		

I'll / I'd be glad to help you, not I'm glad to help you.

Words you need

to inconvenience s.o. jmd. Umstände bereiten
interruption Unterbrechung, Störung
receipt Beleg
to refund erstatten
teller Bankkassierer/in

The pronunciation of receipt is ri-seet, with a silent p.

4 🔊22 **Listen to the audio from Exercise 3 again, and complete the sentences from the dialogues.**

1 What .... to be the ....?

2 I'm .... to .... that.

3 First of all, ... for the poor service.

4 I .... the stress you must be feeling.

5 I'm sorry you've been so ....

6 So, ... how I can

.... you.

7 It .... that our shop assistant made

a ....

8 I'll be happy to .... your money.

9 That's no .... I'll ....

to help you.

👥 Practice reading the transcript with a partner.

> In problems and complaints, we often soften bad news by using phrases such as:
>
> *I'm afraid (that)* your order is going to be late.
> *It seems (that)* they forgot to enclose the instructions.
> *It appears (that)* there's been a misunderstanding.
>
> We can also combine these phrases with the passive tense to acknowledge the problem without saying who exactly made the mistake.
>
> *I'm afraid (that)* your message *got overlooked* somehow.
> *It seems (that)* the order *was not handled* promptly enough.
> *It appears (that)* a mistake *has been made*.

5 **Write a customer-friendly statement for each situation.**

1 You're wrong. Our information is right, not yours.

....

2 It wasn't my colleague's fault that you didn't get the order.

....

3 The company didn't put all the parts in the shipment.

....

4 I didn't get your email, so it's obvious that you didn't send it.

....

5 You won't get the order this week.

....

6 **Read the messages posted on Twitter between a guest and a hotel manager.**

Tweets

George Smith @SmithGeorge   9 mins
Don't ever stay at the BizHotel! I've had it with their terrible service. They don't clean the rooms! Calling them about it is pointless.

Tweets

BIZ HOTEL **BizHotel** @BizHotel   17 mins
@SmithGeorge Hello, can I call you today about your stay in our hotel? I'm sure we can take care of this problem. We value your business!

Words you need
to have had it die Nase voll haben, etw. satt haben
pointless zwecklos

Now complete the dialogues between the guest and the manager with words and phrases from the list.

> follow · I'll be glad · inconvenienced · lodge · make sure · repeat ·
> seemed · terribly · troubled · would you mind

Manager: Hello, Mr. Smith. I'm calling about your tweet. I can see

you're very ....¹ about your last stay
at our hotel.

Guest: Indeed I am! That's why I simply had to

....² a complaint about your hotel
on Twitter.

Manager: So, what ....³ to be the problem, sir?

Guest: Well, I'm a regular guest at your hotel, but I'm ready
to change my mind about ever staying there again!
The service was awful. I had to call housekeeping
every day to ask them to clean my room. I pay good rates to stay at your hotel, so dependable
cleaning service is the least I expect!

Manager: First of all, I'd like to say how ....⁴ sorry I am. I can understand how this

must have ruined your stay with us. So, if I ....⁵ you correctly, you had to

phone each day to get your room serviced? ....⁶ giving me some details?
If I could just get your full name and your room number, what time you called, and who exactly
you spoke to …

* * *

Manager: Mr. Smith, I've just spoken to housekeeping. We really apologize for the poor service. I'd like to

....⁷ this never happens again. Since you have been so ....⁸

by this incident, ...⁹ to offer you two free nights for your next visit at our hotel.
In fact, I'll email you a voucher right now. You can use it any time you wish. We do want to

keep you as a ....¹⁰ customer!

Guest: Oh, that's just great! I am so glad that we could work this out. I do want to keep coming back
to your hotel – the service is usually very good. Thanks for responding to my tweet so quickly.

Words you need

awful/terrible furchtbar
compensation Entschädigung
dependable zuverlässig
incident Zwischenfall
to lodge einreichen
troubled aufgewühlt
voucher Gutschein

◁) 23 Listen to check your answers. Then work with a group to formulate three complaints.
Pair up with another group and respond to one another's complaints using language you've learned.

7 How did the hotel manager deal with the problem in Exercise 6? Read the dialogue again and find
phrases the manager used to respond to the complaint.

1 Apologizing: ....

2 Understanding the problem: ....

3 Following up: ....

4 Giving compensation: ....

What are some other ways to compensate a customer?

8 Problem and complaint procedures in any company require professional language.
Match the headings to the phrases in the flow chart.

> a Apologize. · b Assure the client of follow-up. · c Clarify the information and repeat the problem
> back to the customer. · d End with a friendly, helpful tone. · e Listen carefully to the customer
> describing the problem. · f Offer an alternative if the customer doesn't accept the solution. ·
> g Say how and when the problem will be solved. · h Show empathy. ·
> i Summarize the discussion. · j Take responsibility for the problem.

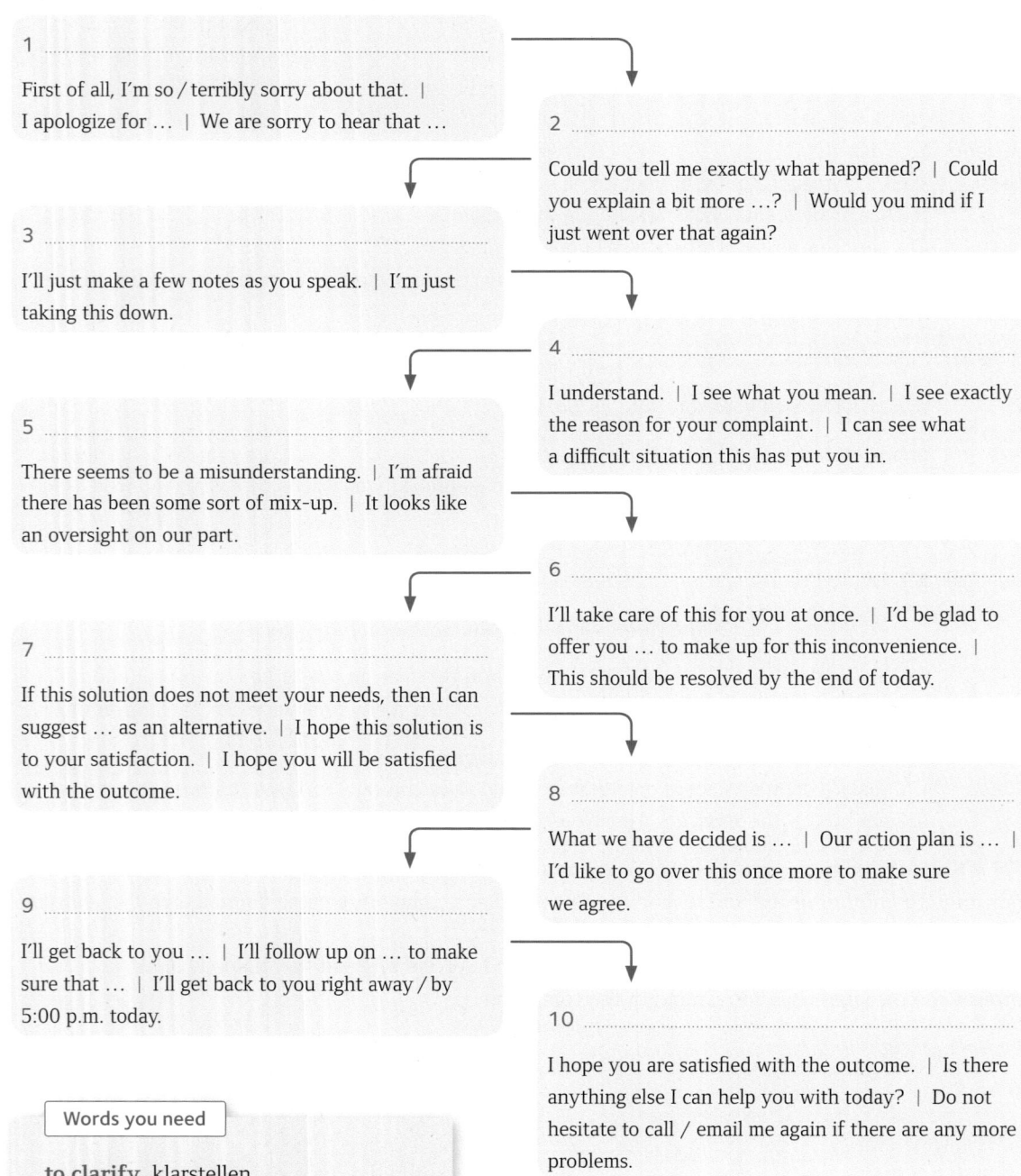

1 ....

First of all, I'm so / terribly sorry about that. |
I apologize for … | We are sorry to hear that …

2 ....

Could you tell me exactly what happened? | Could
you explain a bit more …? | Would you mind if I
just went over that again?

3 ....

I'll just make a few notes as you speak. | I'm just
taking this down.

4 ....

I understand. | I see what you mean. | I see exactly
the reason for your complaint. | I can see what
a difficult situation this has put you in.

5 ....

There seems to be a misunderstanding. | I'm afraid
there has been some sort of mix-up. | It looks like
an oversight on our part.

6 ....

I'll take care of this for you at once. | I'd be glad to
offer you … to make up for this inconvenience. |
This should be resolved by the end of today.

7 ....

If this solution does not meet your needs, then I can
suggest … as an alternative. | I hope this solution is
to your satisfaction. | I hope you will be satisfied
with the outcome.

8 ....

What we have decided is … | Our action plan is … |
I'd like to go over this once more to make sure
we agree.

9 ....

I'll get back to you … | I'll follow up on … to make
sure that … | I'll get back to you right away / by
5:00 p.m. today.

10 ....

I hope you are satisfied with the outcome. | Is there
anything else I can help you with today? | Do not
hesitate to call / email me again if there are any more
problems.

> **Words you need**
>
> **to clarify** klarstellen
> **empathy** Einfühlungsvermögen

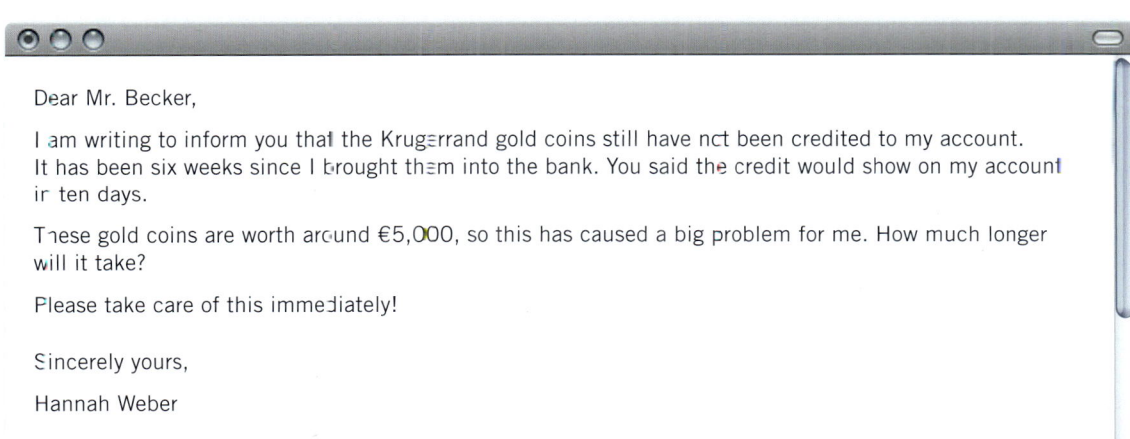

Phrases to use

Once again, we apologize for the inconvenience.

We are very concerned to hear that …

We very much regret …

Dealing with complaints in writing (formal)

The problem has now been resolved.

We do value your business and hope to keep you as a long-term customer.

We assure you that we are doing everything we can.

9 Read the complaint email. Then choose the right words to complete the apology email. Use language from Exercise 8 to help you.

Dear Mr. Becker,

I am writing to inform you that the Krugerrand gold coins still have not been credited to my account. It has been six weeks since I brought them into the bank. You said the credit would show on my account in ten days.

These gold coins are worth around €5,000, so this has caused a big problem for me. How much longer will it take?

Please take care of this immediately!

Sincerely yours,

Hannah Weber

Dear Ms. Weber,

am **apologize / terribly** [1] sorry about the delay in crediting the gold coins to your account. I understand what a difficult situation this **has put / has followed** [2] you in. Unfortunately, it looks like an **inconvenience / oversight** [3] on our part.

I have just spoken to our Frankfurt office. The problem should be **resolved / hesitated** [4] by the end of the day. I will **put / follow up** [5] on this and **make sure / am sure** [6] your account is credited.

As **satisfaction / compensation** [7] for the **solution / inconvenience** [8], I would like to offer you zero service charge on your checking account for the next quarter. I will also be sending you a complimentary briefcase.

I do hope you will be **satisfied / sorry** [9] with the outcome. Do not **apologize / hesitate** [10] to contact me if I can be of further assistance.

Yours sincerely,

Mark Becker

Bank Officer

Apology emails should always be written in a formal style to show seriousness and respect to the customer, no matter how well you know the customer.

Would you follow up this email response to a customer's complaint with a phone call or meeting? With a partner, discuss situations in which you need to use different kinds of communication to solve a customer problem.

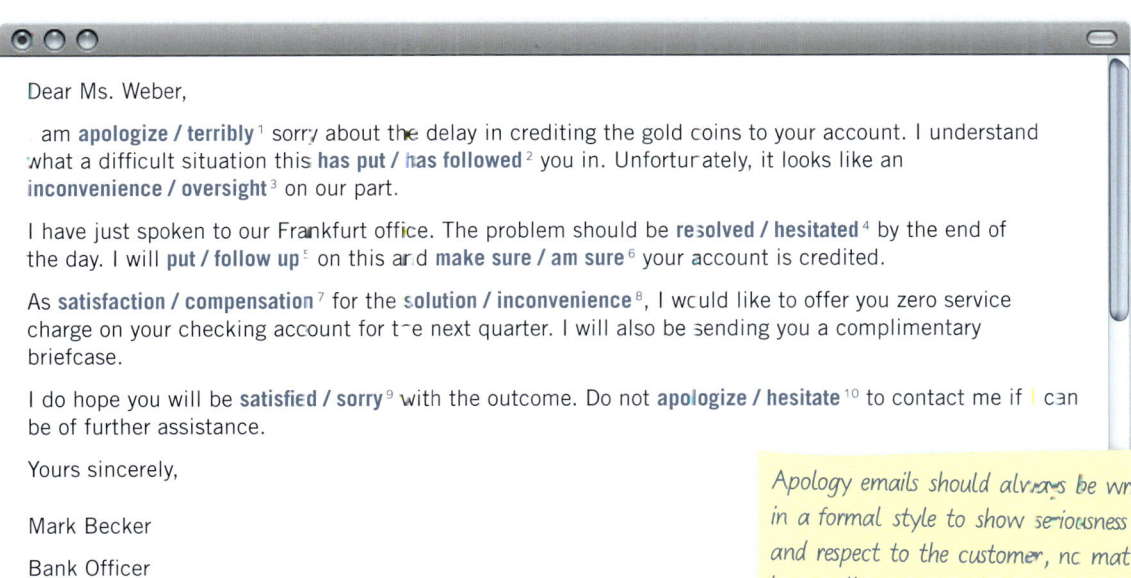

10 What's wrong with the following answers to customers' complaints? How do you think the customer would react in each case?

1 I don't really deal with that. That's not my department.
2 Oh, that's not a problem (when it is one).
3 We can't help you with that.
4 I don't know.
5 We don't give refunds – as soon as you leave the store, it's yours.

Here are more professional answers and explanations of complaint policies. Match 1–5 with a–e below.

☐ a We have an exchange policy, but unfortunately refunds are not possible. So, please make your selection carefully before buying. Can I help you decide which product would be best for you?
☐ b I can give you some general advice, but it would be better if you spoke to my colleague. He's the specialist in this area. May I transfer you to him?
☐ c I'm really not certain about that, but I'll find out for you. I'll call you back by 4:00 today. Is that OK?
☐ d I'm afraid this isn't something our company offers. I can recommend that you contact Fritz GmbH, which does offer that product.
☐ e That sounds like something we could do for you. May I ask my manager about it and call you back?

Tell a partner about a policy in your company. Practice explaining it in a polite, positive way.

11 How do people in similar jobs in other countries deal with complaints? Do you think there are cultural differences in the way customers complain and what they complain about? How about the way complaints are dealt with and apologies are made?

12

Simulation

Consider two common customer complaints you receive at work. Make notes on how you would resolve the problems and respond to the customers in English. Would you contact the customers by phone or email, in face-to-face meetings, or by using social media? Are there company policies you need to explain to the customers?

Use the form on the right to make notes.

Complaint 1:...
....
....
....
Complaint 2:...
....
....
....

The Customer Care Forum

Home | Membership | Training and Events | Articles and Issues | Contact Us

Home | **Articles and Issues**

The Impact of Facebook and Twitter on Customer Care

Dealing with complaints and problems from customers has taken on a new dimension with social media platforms. A story about a good or bad experience with customer service is no longer confined to one person and his/her
5   circle of friends. Facebook and Twitter are now popular routes for commenting on customer service. Customers can report a problem with a company publicly. If a company doesn't resolve a problem to a customer's satisfaction, it isn't just losing a customer. It's also potentially facing
10 a public relations disaster.

Facebook and Twitter also make commenting on a company's products and services faster and easier. Customers can post complaints quickly and with little effort.

Surveys have suggested that one negative comment on Facebook or one bad tweet on Twitter can lose a business up to 30 customers. Typically, a negative review by a customer on one of
15 these major social media sites reaches 45 people. Of these, 30 people will not purchase anything from a company they've heard bad things about.

So how can companies deal with complaints made via social media? Just ignore or dismiss them as trendy communication hype? That's no longer possible – these technologies are here to stay. The only solution from a business viewpoint is for companies to develop their own
20 systems for monitoring social media. It's becoming crucial to know when someone says something bad about a company or its services. Without a proactive strategy in place to track such comments, a company is at risk. Nowadays a business can't afford to underestimate the ability of negative comments on social media to affect its customer base.

25 Thus customer service experts should realize that the time to fully integrate services from social media platforms is sooner rather than later. A few years down the road, a company without a social media strategy will look dated and odd – almost like a company with no website!

Words you need	
confined to	beschränkt auf
crucial	ausschlaggebend
dated	veraltet, überholt
to dismiss sth.	etw. abtun
to purchase	kaufen
to suggest	nahelegen
to underestimate	unterschätzen

Over to you

- What kind of impact have Facebook and Twitter had on your company?
- Does your company monitor these platforms? How does it follow up on complaints posted to them? How fast are the issues resolved?
- With a partner, share an experience you've had with complaints and problems on Facebook and Twitter.

Transcripts

Unit 1   **Exercise 8**   ◁ 02

For any customer care job at our company, you must be fluent in German and English and have a very good telephone manner and excellent customer service skills. PC skills, as well as good communication skills, are essential.

Not only that, it's really important to be able to perform under pressure and to show good follow-through.

At any time, really, our customer care employees have to provide customers with first-class service – in all kinds of communications. A customer care agent can deal with inquiries and handle problems and complaints. Superior writing and speaking skills are a must in our customer service jobs.

We also need people who can manage a lot of teamwork – both internally and externally at our company. This requires clear communication skills with both colleagues and customers. Throughout any contact, the person must show tact and diplomacy.

Unit 1   **Exercise 10**   ◁ 03

1 Your company employees are impatient. They never wait for people to finish what they have to say.
2 The customer service agents are always polite and friendly. They always take time to help me and answer my questions.
3 Why aren't your secretaries more attentive on the phone? They don't listen, and they aren't interested in customers at all.
4 Your call center agents are really helpful and efficient.
5 The hotel concierge is very knowledgeable about sightseeing information.
6 Your colleague was inefficient and seemed to take a long time to process my order.
7 The clerk was really rude and acted like he didn't see me.
8 The waiter was well informed about the menu and brought our food fast.
9 The employees at the reception desk were inattentive and made me wait to be checked in.
10 The call center agent was very patient and explained everything to me again.

Unit 2   **Exercise 3**   ◁ 04

1 We're happy to have you here.
d Thanks, I'm glad to be here, too.
2 How do you do?
a How do you do?
3 Let me introduce myself. I'm Roger Becker. I'm head of sales.

b Nice to meet you. My name's Martina Wolf. I'm in advertising.
4 Have you met? Marcus this is Olivia.
c Oh, no, we haven't. So nice to meet you.
5 How are you?
e Fine, thanks, and you?

Unit 2   **Exercise 7**   ◁ 05

A Would you care to come this way? Our meeting room is just down the corridor.
B Fine, I'll follow you.
A May I take your coat? I'll hang it on the coatrack for you.
B Thanks, that'd be very kind of you.
A Please have a seat. Can I bring you a cup of coffee or tea?
B Oh, coffee sounds fine.
A How do you like your coffee?
B Just black, please.

Unit 2   **Exercise 13**   ◁ 06

A Where are you from originally?
B I was born and grew up in Houston, Texas.
C So, how did you get into this line of business?
D I did an internship program at …
E What do you do in your free time?
F I enjoy playing tennis and going to classical music concerts.
G Have you ever been to Vienna before?
H Well, I've been to Austria twice, but I'm not really familiar with Vienna.
I Have you tried our local cuisine?
J Yes, but I only know Wienerschnitzel and Apfelstrudel. What else can you recommend for me to try?
K Would you like to join us for drinks after the meeting?
L Yes, I'd love to. Could we go to one of your famous wine cellars? I've heard you've got very good white wine.

Unit 3   **Exercise 2**   ◁ 07

SR Sales Representative
NC New Customer

Welcoming a customer, offering hospitality, and getting down to business
SR So nice to see you again. Would you like something to drink?
NC Yes, please. I'll take a black coffee.
SR So, shall we get down to business? As I understand from our emails and phone calls, you're interested in our office equipment offers.

NC Yes, that's right. However, to start, I do have some direct questions about your customer service. Would you mind if I asked them now?

SR Not at all, go ahead.

NC How will I be able to see that you're keeping your service commitment to us?

SR Well, that's a really important point. We follow up on customer satisfaction by regular contact. This means by email, phone, meetings, or even video-conferencing – whichever you prefer.

NC How often do you upgrade your products and services?

SR We normally launch our upgrades every six months. We would inform you of upgrades before providing them to the general market. You would receive special offers on these upgrades.

NC Thanks for clearing that up. Now I'd really like to take a closer look at your range of photocopiers.

SR All right. I'd be glad to go over that for you.

Wrapping up the meeting and saying goodbye to a customer

SR So, I think we can wrap up our discussion. We've outlined the products you'd like to order. I'll get them in the contract so you can review the details. Would that be OK?

NC Yes, that sounds fine.

SR We'll contact you again by next Monday. Do you use Skype or another type of video link? I could contact you that way, if that's convenient for you

NC Email is the best way to reach me.

SR All right, then. Thanks for such a good meeting. Have a nice trip back home!

NC Thank you for your kind help. Goodbye!

Unit 3   Exercise 7   ◁ 08

Inviting the customer

A Would you like to join us for drinks and dinner?

B Oh, sure, I'd like that very much.

A We have a number of good restaurants nearby. What sort of cuisine do you prefer?

B I really like Greek or Mediterranean style food.

A Great, there's a good Greek restaurant around the corner.

At the restaurant

A So, what can I get you to drink?

B I'll have a white wine, please.

A Please order what you'd like for dinner. It's on us since you're a special customer!

B Well, I appreciate that. I'd like the moussaka and an olive and tomato salad.

A So, have you had the chance to do any sightseeing in Munich?

B Not yet, but I'd really like to see some art museums tomorrow. What do you suggest?

A I highly recommend the Pinakothek Museums. They've got all kinds of art – from the Old Masters to the Expressionists.

B Sounds fascinating. I think I'll go over there tomorrow morning.

Unit 3   Exercise 10   ◁ 09

Q I make presentations quite a bit in my job. I feel comfortable doing a basic presentation to customers. I can describe products and services really well. The problem begins when I meet customers after the talk. I'm not confident in dealing with the question and answer, or Q&A, session. What if I can't answer their questions? Also, I'm not the best at making small talk after my talk. I know I'm risking making a negative impression on customers. Any tips for me?

A I completely understand your situation. We might have the presentation basics down, but social interaction in and around the talk can be tricky. First, the Q&A session is very important to show your customer-focused attitude. Be well-prepared with information on your products and services. However, don't be afraid to say you don't have an answer to a question. Let customers know you'll be in touch later with an answer. Your attentive follow-up by phone or email about their question could be the first step in establishing contact with a new customer!

Mingling after your presentation can make a definite impact on customers. Just talk in a relaxed and friendly manner. Be open-minded and curious, and get their feedback on the presentation. I think customers want to see how well you listen to their ideas and concerns. The more you focus on customers in all your small talk, the more confident you'll feel. This projects a good customer care image for both you and your company.

Unit 3   Exercise 14   ◁ 10

A I'd like to introduce myself. I'm Otto Brandt. I work for Metro GmbH. May I ask your name?

B So, Mr. Gillan, how are you enjoying the trade fair?

C Well, then, are you looking for anything in particular?

D OK, but please feel free to ask me any questions I'd be glad to go over our products and try to find something suitable for your company.

E Ah, can I interest you in our latest brochure? It has information about our company and our full range of products.

F Would you like to put your name on our mailing list?

G Would you mind if I took your business card? I'll make sure you're on our list. And here's my card with full contact details. I'll send you a quick email next week to see if I can help you with any of our products

Unit 4   Exercise 1   ◁ 11

Call 1

Agent Yeah?

Marjorie Hello. This is Marjorie Heighton. I'd like to confirm my appointment with Peter Gore.

Agent Um … Sorry, what did you say?

Marjorie I'd like to confirm my appointment with Peter Gore, please.

Agent Well, this is the wrong number for that. Uh, wait … Hello? Ms. … um, Hate …?

Marjorie Heighton. Marjorie Heighton.

Agent Look, I'm not responsible for that. You'll have to call Peter's secretary.

Marjorie OK. Can you give me the phone number or connect me?

Agent Yeah, OK. Does anyone know Peter's extension?

Call 2

Martha Hello, Martha Greer speaking. May I help you?

Donald Hello, this is Donald Kraft. Could I speak to Anthony Smithson, please?

Martha Sorry, could you repeat that, please?

Donald Yes, this is Donald Kraft. I'd like to speak to Anthony Smithson.

Martha I'm afraid you've got the wrong extension, Mr. Kraft. You need to speak to Mr. Smithson's office. Would you like me to connect you?

Donald Yes, that would be great.

Martha OK, Mr. Kraft. I'm putting you through now. Thanks for your call.

Unit 4 **Exercise 2** ◁ 12

Call 1

Elke Good morning, Apex Industries. May I help you?

John Yes, this is John Richards from Customer Software Services. I'd like to speak to Eva Lang, please.

Elke Of course, just a moment, please … Oh, it seems that her line is busy. Could you hold for a moment? Or would you like to leave a message?

John I'd prefer to hold for just a minute or two.

Elke OK, she'll be with you soon.

Elke Mr. Richards, thanks for holding. I'm putting you through to Ms. Lang's office now. If you get cut off for some reason, please call again.

John I'm sorry. Could you speak up a bit? I didn't catch that.

Elke Sure. I'm connecting you now to Ms. Lang's office. If you don't get through, please call again.

Call 2

Elke Good morning, Apex Industries.

John This is John Richards again. I'm afraid I got cut off when you tried to put me through.

Elke I'm terribly sorry about that.

John I really need to get through to Ms. Lang this afternoon. Could I leave a message for her?

Elke Yes certainly, Mr. Richards. Could I have your phone number?

John Yes, I'm calling from my cell phone. It's country code +1, then 408 555 3392.

Elke Right. So, that's country code +1, 408 555 3392. I'll make sure she calls you back today. Can I help you with anything else?

John Would it be possible to have her cell phone number? Could you perhaps look it up for me?

Elke Yes, that's no problem. It's in our directory. It's +49 for Germany then 152 288 17386.

John 152 288 17386. Thanks once again. Bye.

Elke You're welcome. Goodbye.

Unit 4 **Exercise 10** ◁ 13

Carol Carol Warner speaking.

Hannah Hi Carol. This is Hannah from Creative Concepts. How are you? How's the weather in Houston?

Carol Oh, hello Hannah. Good to hear from you. I'm fine. It's still a bit warm here. Anyway, what can I do for you today?

Hannah Could we arrange a meeting for next week? How about Thursday at 10:00 a.m.?

Carol Sorry, I'm a bit tied up on Thursday. Could we meet Wednesday at 2:00 p.m. instead?

Hannah Yes, I'm available then. Where would be the best place to meet?

Carol Well, I'll pencil in the conference room. Let me confirm that with you by 5:00 p.m. today.

Hannah Sounds good. Could you email me the confirmation? I'll be difficult to reach by phone the rest of the day.

Carol Sure, no problem.

Hannah Well, look forward to seeing you at the meeting. Bye.

Carol Likewise! See you then. Goodbye.

Unit 4 **Exercise 13** ◁ 14

Jon Hello, this is Jon Marshal. I can't answer the phone right now. Please leave a message, and I'll return your call as soon as possible.

Barbara Hello Jon. This is Barbara Kennedy calling. About our appointment next week, something has come up. I'm afraid I can't make it on Monday. I'll be tied up all day. Could we postpone the meeting to Tuesday at 10:00 a.m.? Please let me know if that's convenient for you. Call me back or email me. Thanks!

Unit 5 **Exercise 1** ◁ 15

Call 1

Customer Hello.

Agent Hello, is this Mr. Anderson?

Customer Yes, speaking.

Agent This is Klaus Heinrich from ModernTech Communications. I'm calling because I got a message that you called our QuickHelp line. It seems that you need some assistance?

Customer Oh, great. Yes, there's a bit of a problem with our bank's IT system. When we try to view our customer accounts, the program crashes …

Agent Mr. Anderson, let me just type this in … one moment … OK. Could you tell me when exactly it crashes?

Customer Well, it's hard to tell what causes it. The normal screen comes up and asks you to type in the name first, then hit return, then type in the password. It seems OK at first, the new page comes up, then there's a funny clicking noise like the computer's trying to do something. This goes on quite a long time, then the screen just freezes.

Agent OK, so, as I understand it, the problem starts when you enter the password. Is that right?

Customer Yes, that's right.

Agent And how long have you had this problem?

Customer Well, I've only tried it twice but then thought I'd better call you. So, when can you take care of this? Our work depends on the system being up and running all the time.

Agent Yes, I can understand how important it is. I think we can send someone out to you this afternoon. I'll check the service technicians' schedule and call you back in half an hour. Does that sound all right?

Customer That sounds good.

Agent OK, and I'll call you when the technician has finished the repair work to make sure everything went well.

Customer Great.

Agent Can I assist you with anything else today?

Customer No, but thanks for asking. I'll be waiting for your call.

Call 2

Agent Good afternoon, Smith Media Concepts. Gerry speaking. How can I help you?

Customer Hello, I'd like to place an order, please. The name's Jochen Wagner. I'm already a regular customer.

Agent Could I have your account number, please?

Customer Mmm, yes, it's 55878.

Agent 55878 … One moment, let me just pull up your customer file on my screen. Right. So, Mr. Wagner, what can I do for you?

Customer I'd like to place an order for some spare parts and was wondering if it would be possible to receive them by Thursday? It's quite urgent.

Agent Well, if the items are in stock, it should be no problem to send them out right away. What exactly would you like to order? Could you give me the first order number, please?

Customer OK, that's EJT53021. I'd like two of them. And the other order number is … EJS36899. I need eight.

Agent Was that E, J, and S as in Sam?

Customer Right.

Agent OK, let me repeat that. E, J, and T, as in Thomas, 53021, two items. And E, J, and S as in Sam, 36899, eight items. Is that correct?

Customer That's right. Are they in stock?

Agent Yes, they are. I'll flag your order as urgent so the items will be sent out right away. You should receive the order in a couple of days, and definitely by Thursday.

Customer Sounds good.

Agent Can I help you with anything else today?

Customer No, that's all for today, thank you.

Agent OK, Mr. Wagner, thank you for your order. Goodbye.

| Unit 5 | Exercise 5 | 16 |

Agent Good morning. Ace Town Beverages Helpline. May I help you?

Customer Yes, please. I need to place an order for ten more cases of my standard house wine.

Agent It sounds like you have ordered from us before. Could you give me your customer number, please?

Customer Of course, here it is … uh … 55008-22.

Agent Ah yes, Mr. Green from Suavo Restaurant. I'd just like to confirm your contact details. So, that's Breitestrasse …

Customer No, that's our old address. We've just moved to Hauptstrasse 43. The zip code is still 45221.

Agent OK, let me just repeat that. That's Hauptstrasse 43, zip code 45221.

Customer Yes, that's right.

Agent OK, I've updated our database. Let me just type in the order … OK …

Customer Look, I'm really in a bind. Could you do a rush order so that we get it by tomorrow morning?

Agent Sure, that's no problem. We can dispatch today for overnight delivery. OK, Mr. Green, could I go over your order again? You'd like your standard order of house wine. And we'll rush the order so it arrives around 10:00 a.m.

Customer Yes, that's correct. Thanks for being so helpful.

Agent Can I help you with anything else?

| Unit 5 | Exercise 6 | 17 |

Alfa	Golf	Mike	Sierra	Yankee
Bravo	Hotel	November	Tango	Zulu
Charlie	India	Oscar	Uniform	
Delta	Juliet	Papa	Victor	
Echo	Kilo	Quebec	Whiskey	
Foxtrot	Lima	Romeo	X-ray	

| Unit 5 | Exercise 8 | 18 |

Operator Hello. Susanne speaking. How can I help you?

Customer Hello. I hope I'm at the right place. I just got a new MP3 player – the i-go. I'm trying to install the software, but it just won't work.

Operator OK, first of all, is that the i-go mini or the i-go maxi?

Customer The mini.

Operator Right. So what exactly is the problem? Could you explain what you've done so far?

Customer Well, I put in the CD to install the software, and it seemed to work.

Operator Right.

Customer But now I can't open the window.

Operator OK.

Customer There's some message about something to do with the system and a number.

Operator I see. It could be a systems requirement problem.

Customer Sorry, what does that mean?

Operator Well, the systems requirement for the i-go is OS 10 version 10.1.4. That means you need to have that version or a more recent one on your computer, or you can't run the software for the i-go.

Customer OK, but what does OS stand for?

Operator That's your operating system, the software that manages your computer.

Customer I see.

Operator So, could you tell me which operating system you have on your computer?

Customer No, sorry. I'm afraid I'm not very good with computers, as you can tell. I got this i-go for Christmas, and I didn't think it would be so difficult to use.

Operator Oh, don't worry. We just need to clarify a few things; then you'll have no trouble. OK, do you see the green box in the upper left-hand corner of your screen?

Customer Uh huh.

Operator When you click on it you'll see a menu. The first item on the menu says "about your computer." Are you following me all right?

Customer Yes.

Operator OK, click on that, and you'll see what operating system you have. Are you having any trouble seeing that? The letters OS followed by some numbers?

Customer Ah … yes, um … it's OS 10.1. Is that what you mean?

Operator That's right, and we've found your problem. You need to upgrade your system before you can install the software for your i-go.

Customer And how do I do that?

Operator Oh, that's very easy. Let me just talk you through the steps …

***

Operator So, that will take a while to download, but once it does, you can just use it to upgrade your system free of charge. Then you'll have no trouble installing the i-go software.

Customer Great. Thanks so much.

Operator You're welcome. By the way, have you registered with us?

Customer No, I don't think so. Could you tell me more about that?

Operator Well, if you register with us, we can activate your guarantee, and you'll have two years of free service …

Unit 5	Exercise 11	◁ 19

Customer I'm having trouble with my cable TV and Internet system. It turns on and seems to work, but I can't get any channels on the TV. Then the Internet icon on my computer says it's connected, but there's still no access.

Agent Oh, I'm so sorry to hear about that. OK, I'm going to need to ask you some questions. Have you tried unplugging the cables and reconnecting them?

Customer Yes, but it still doesn't seem to work.

Agent How about turning the main system box for the TV and Internet on and off?

Customer I've tried that as well. I've also pushed every button on the remote control to at least get something moving on the TV.

Agent Well, it sounds like we really need to send out a technician. In the meantime, I'd recommend not using the remote control for the TV. When would be a convenient time to set up an appointment?

Customer Is there any way I can watch any TV until then?

Agent Why don't you switch off the cable box and just watch the local channels?

Customer Thanks very much. I'll do that!

Unit 6	Exercise 11	◁ 20

Radio Host Good morning. We are speaking today to Dr. Gerald Vaught, a business communication specialist. He has recently conducted a study into the impact of textspeak: the language of texting and tweeting and its effect on good writing in the workplace. So, Dr. Vaught, texting and tweeting seem to be quickly replacing emails and even telephone calls. What does your research show about its effect on business communication?

Dr. Vaught Well, as you and your listeners likely know, this type of language is the opposite of high quality, formal writing. It uses shortcuts like abbreviations and acronyms to communicate messages quickly. It has some practical uses, such as communicating basic facts quickly. What we've discovered, however, is that even within the conventions for textspeak, its users are sloppier in all their writing than more conventional writers that do not use the language.

Radio Host That's interesting. But, business people are always in a hurry. As long as the message can be understood and can be written quickly, does it matter if there are errors in it?

Dr. Vaught Well, yes and no. On the one hand, there is a good rationale for being brief and succinct. However, we can't assume that such messages are easy to understand. For instance, my research found that younger workers had an easier time deciphering these kinds of messages. But even then the workers needed more time to understand the meaning of the poorly written messages than to understand those that had been written well. So the question is, whose time is being saved? Clearly the writer's time, but not always the recipient's.

Radio Host OK, what about, say, text messages written within the conventions for texting? In other words, messages that use some well established and understood shortcuts. Some argue that this kind of thing in language has a positive effect because it's a way in which language is changing to suit the times.

Dr. Vaught It's true that innovation in language isn't necessarily dangerous. But in the case of business communication, we've found that those who use textspeak are more likely to write poorly or to simply be indifferent to proper business writing.

Radio Host Wow, OK. Do you mean that these writers might be losing the ability to write correctly?

Dr. Vaught Possibly. But the evidence points to less interest in writing well. Their writing is also generally more informal, even in situations that call for a more formal style of writing.

Radio Host I see. I presume this can have a negative effect on business relationships?

Dr. Vaught That's correct. One of the major findings of my study is that too much textspeak negatively affects business relationships. There is a use for such language in business. Indeed, business people might need to use it if they have, for instance, a client who uses it heavily. But it needs to be differentiated from proper communication.

Radio Host Well, this sounds like something that we all might need to think about these days. Thank you for being with us today, Dr. Vaught.

| Unit 7 | Exercise 1 | ◁ 21 |

Recently we've been getting a lot of complaints from customers who're annoyed with the quality of our customer service. Here're just three of the comments we've received: "I had a problem with one of your services. When I told the employee about it, he was condescending and arrogant and acted like my problem was stupid and unimportant. He even suggested the problem was my fault."

And another: "The person on the phone didn't even listen to what I was saying. I had to repeat myself two or three times. Then she just said, 'Well, that's our company policy. I can't do anything about how we do our business.' She didn't even apologize!"

And a third: "I realize I was angry and perhaps spoke sharply, but the receptionist didn't have to shout at me. She told me it wasn't her mistake and that I should speak to the person who caused the problem, not her."

At our next staff meeting, we need to discuss our complaints procedure and how we can improve our customer care. I would like you all to make an action checklist on how to improve the way we resolve problems and present your ideas at the meeting.

| Unit 7 | Exercise 3 | ◁ 22 |

Dialogue 1

Customer Excuse me. I'd like to make a complaint.

Bank Manager Oh, I'm sorry to hear that. What seems to be the problem?

Customer Your bank service is just awful. I was here last week to take care of some banking transactions. The line was very long since there was only one teller. I asked a bank employee to bring in another teller, but he said they were too busy with more important work. So it took me over an hour to get my business done. I'm going to change to the Clyde Bank!

Bank Manager First of all, let me apologize for the poor service and unhelpful employees. It seems that you went through a terrible time getting your business

done. Why don't you come into my office where we can talk without any interruptions?

Dialogue 2

Customer You really need to help me! My flight to Manchester has been canceled. This is a huge problem for me since I have to get there by tomorrow at 10:00 a.m. for an important meeting. If I don't get there in time, I could lose a very special client! I'm a frequent flier with your airline, so I expect you to do something about this right away.

Airline Agent I understand the stress you must be feeling. I'm afraid we've had to cancel several flights today due to weather, and I'm sorry you've been so inconvenienced. So, let me see how I can assist you …

Dialogue 3

Customer Excuse me. I bought this sweater at your shop yesterday. When I got home, I looked at the receipt and saw that you had overcharged me by €10.

Floor Manager Oh, I'm so sorry. It appears that our shop assistant made a mistake. I'll be happy to refund your money.

Customer Actually, I've also decided that the sweater isn't really the right color, so I'd like to exchange it for the red and yellow one.

Floor Manager That's no problem. I'll be glad to help you.

| Unit 7 | Exercise 6 | ◁ 23 |

Manager Hello, Mr. Smith. I'm calling about your tweet. I can see you're very troubled about your last stay at our hotel.

Guest Indeed I am! That's why I simply had to lodge a complaint about your hotel on Twitter.

Manager So, what seemed to be the problem, sir?

Guest Well, I'm a regular guest at your hotel, but I'm ready to change my mind about ever staying there again! The service was awful. I had to call housekeeping every day to ask them to clean my room. I pay good rates to stay at your hotel, so dependable cleaning service is the least I expect!

Manager First of all, I'd like to say how terribly sorry I am. I can understand how this must have ruined your stay with us. So, if I follow you correctly, you had to phone each day to get your room serviced? Would you mind giving me some details? If I could just get your full name and your room number, what time you called, and who exactly you spoke to …

***

Manager Mr. Smith, I've just spoken to housekeeping. We really apologize for the poor service. I'd like to make sure this never happens again. Since you have been so inconvenienced by this incident, I'll be glad to offer you two free nights for your next visit at our hotel. In fact, I'll email you a voucher right now. You can use it any time you wish. We do want to keep you as a repeat customer!

Guest Oh, that's just great! I am so glad that we could work this out. I do want to keep coming back to your hotel – the service is usually very good. Thanks for responding to my tweet so quickly.

Answer Key

Unit 1 ....

Warmer
Answers will vary.

Exercise 1
makes shopping online simple and convenient | customers can easily find everything they need, make inquiries, track orders, and return purchases | large product range | good online interactions | good assistance over the phone | excellent in meeting the needs of its customers

Exercise 2
1 satisfaction 2 aim 3 assistance 4 excellent 5 to trust
6 simple, convenient

Exercise 3
1 convenience 2 trust 3 assistance 4 aim 5 satisfaction

Exercise 4
Answers will vary.

Exercise 5
1 sales assistant 2 clerk 3 cashier 4 hotel 5 receptionist
6 restaurant 7 order entry clerk 8 sales

Exercise 6
1 c 2 a 3 b 4 e 5 d

Exercise 7
Answers will vary.

Exercise 8
1 fluent 2 manner 3 PC skills 4 communication
5 perform under pressure 6 follow-through
7 deal with inquiries 8 handle 9 complaints 10 writing
11 teamwork 12 tact

Exercise 9
Possible answers

People skills
2 excellent customer service
3 good communication
4 superior writing and speaking abilities
5 work well in a team

Business skills
2 perform well under pressure
3 deal with inquiries well
4 good follow-through
5 handle problems and complaints well

Exercise 10
1 N 2 P 3 N 4 P 5 P 6 N 7 N 8 P 9 N 10 P

Exercise 11
1 c 2 e 3 a 4 d 5 b

Exercise 12
1 polite 2 attentive 3 efficient 4 knowledgeable
5 patient

Exercise 13
Answers will vary.

Exercise 14
Answers will vary.

Unit 2 ....

Warmer
Answers will vary.

Exercise 1
Possible answers
I take his/her coat.
I offer him/her something to drink.
I ask him/her if he/she found the office OK.

Exercise 2
A Greeting the customer
B Saying your name and meeting for the first time
C Saying the name of your colleague

Exercise 3
1 d 2 a 3 b 4 c 5 e

Exercise 4
Answers will vary.

Exercise 5
1 How are you? 2 Great to see you again!
3 How are things going? 4 How's business?

Exercise 6
Answers will vary.

Exercise 7
1 Would 2 care 3 corridor 4 I'll follow 5 May 6 take
7 I'll hang 8 coatrack 9 Thanks 10 have 11 Can
12 sounds 13 like 14 Just

Exercise 8
1 flight / turbulence/punctual 2 flight / turbulence/punctual
3 punctual / trip 4 punctual / trip 5 drive / traffic jam
6 drive / traffic jam

Exercise 9
1 drive 2 traffic 3 flight 4 turbulence 5 trip 6 punctual

Exercise 10
1 e 2 a 3 d 4 b 5 c

Exercise 11
1 find 2 pleasant 3 like 4 uncomfortable 5 bothers
6 stand

Exercise 12
Answers will vary.

Exercise 13

1 originally 2 was born 3 grew up 4 line of business
5 internship 6 do you do 7 enjoy 8 ever 9 familiar
10 cuisine 11 recommend 12 join 13 cellars

Exercise 14

Good	Taboo
travel	religion
weather	health
current news headlines	someone's weight
accommodation	money
free time activities	sex
home town or country	age
customer's job	politics

Exercise 15

Answers will vary.

Exercise 16

1 coming 2 pleasure 3 forward 4 keep 5 Take 6 Have

Exercise 17

Possible answers

1 Welcome to … / I'd like to welcome you to … / We're pleased/delighted to welcome you to … / We're glad/happy to have you here …
2 Would you care to come this way? Our meeting room is just down the corridor.
3 Can I take your coat/hat/umbrella? / I'll hang your coat on the coatrack for you.
4 Please take a seat.
5 Can I bring you a cup of coffee or tea?
6 How was your flight?
7 Where are you staying? / How's your hotel? / Do you have a room with a view? / Is the hotel in a convenient location? / How's the breakfast buffet?
8 Would you like to join us for lunch in the employee cafeteria?
9 Where are you from originally?
10 Thanks so much for coming. / It was a pleasure to meet you. / Look forward to seeing you again next week. / Please keep in touch. / Goodbye. Take care. / Have a good flight.

Unit 3

Warmer
Answers will vary.

Exercise 1

1 b 2 a 3 e 4 c 5 d

Exercise 2

1 shall 2 get down 3 mind 4 commitment
5 satisfaction 6 upgrade 7 launch 8 inform 9 range
10 go over 11 wrap up 12 convenient

Exercise 3

Possible answers

3 How often do you do customer surveys?
4 How quickly do you deal with customer complaints? (What's your turnaround time for complaints?)

5 What are some examples of compensation you can offer a customer?

Exercise 4

Possible answers

2 What's your hometown like?
3 What do you think of the weather today?
4 Have you been (to Berlin) before?

Exercise 5

1 are you 2 Oh, really 3 How interesting 4 isn't it
5 is it

Exercise 6

1 e 2 c 3 f 4 a 5 d 6 b

Exercise 7

1 join 2 cuisine 3 get 4 I'll have 5 on us 6 appreciate
7 sightseeing 8 suggest

Exercise 8

1 Would you like to join us for dinner?
2 What can I get you to drink?
3 It's on us.
4 I'll have a whiskey, please.
5 I'd like a schnitzel and French fries.

Exercise 9

Answers will vary.

Exercise 10

1 F 2 T 3 F 4 T 5 F

Exercise 11

1 Let me try to answer some of your questions.
2 Could you give me some background on your company?
3 I'll look into that for you.
4 Could you leave me your business card? Here's my card with my complete contact details.
5 Would you mind signing the list?
6 Why don't we get in touch next week?

Exercise 12

Possible answers

1 So, how long have you been with your company?
2 What would you like to see while you're in town?
3 What exact product or service specifications are you looking for?

Exercise 13

Answers will vary.

Exercise 14

1 introduce 2 ask 3 enjoying 4 particular 5 free 6 glad
7 suitable 8 brochure 9 put 10 mind 11 make sure
12 email

Exercise 15

1 May I ask your name?
2 Are you looking for anything in particular?
3 Please feel free to ask me any questions.
4 Can I interest you in our latest brochure?
5 Would you like to put your name on our mailing list?
6 Would you mind if I took your business card?
7 I'll send you a quick email next week.

Exercise 16
Answers will vary.

....

Warmer
Answers will vary; however, it's good to put all of these points into practice when talking to customers on the phone.

Exercise 1
Speaker A in Call 1 made a bad impression, and Speaker A in Call 2 made a good impression.

What went right	What went wrong
In Call 2, Speaker A spoke formally and politely. Though she wasn't able to help Speaker B, she offered to transfer him to the person who could.	In Call 1, Speaker A did not speak formally or politely or offer to help Speaker B reach the person she wished to speak to.

1 May I help you? 2 you repeat that, please 3 I'm afraid 4 Would you like me 5 Thanks for your call

Exercise 2
1 May I help you 2 just a moment 3 would you like 4 thanks for holding 5 catch 6 I'm afraid 7 terribly sorry 8 Yes certainly 9 I'll make sure 10 no problem

Exercise 3
1 c 2 e 3 d 4 a 5 g 6 b 7 h 8 f

Exercise 4
1 look up 2 speak up 3 cut off 4 get through 5 get back to 6 put me through

Exercise 5
Answers will vary.

Exercise 6
1 Identifying yourself
2 Saying why you're calling
3 Showing follow-up
4 Showing attention
5 Understanding the caller
6 Summarizing
7 Giving action points
8 Assuring the caller
9 Wrapping up with the customer

Exercise 7
1 b 2 c 3 a 4 h 5 e 6 d 7 g 8 f

Exercise 8
1 Asking 2 Agreeing / Deciding 3 Suggesting 4 Deciding / Agreeing 5 Confirming 6 Apologizing

Exercise 9
1 c 2 d 3 e 4 a 5 b

Exercise 10
1 speaking 2 weather 3 can 4 set up / arrange / schedule / fix 5 How / What 6 tied up 7 available / free 8 pencil in / reserve 9 confirm 10 reach

Exercise 11
Answers will vary.

Exercise 12
1 make 2 important 3 comfortable 4 arrange 5 cancel

Exercise 13
1 come up 2 can't make 3 tied up 4 postpone 5 convenient

Exercise 14
Answers will vary.

....

Warmer
1 24% 2 11% 3 16% 4 7% 5 62%

Exercise 1

	Call 1	Call 2
Customer	Mr. Anderson from a bank	Jochen Wagner, a regular customer
Customer interested in	He would like help with bank's IT system.	He would like to place an order for some spare parts.
Follow-up	Agent will call back in half an hour and may send out a technician.	Agent will send the order out right away.

Exercise 2
1 It seems 2 Let me just 3 I understand 4 I'll check, call you back 5 pull up 6 I'll flag 7 Thank you

Exercise 3
1 Signal a friendly ready-to-help attitude with your tone and voice.
How can I help you?
It seems that you need some assistance?
What can I do for you?

2 Show that you are listening carefully.
OK, let me repeat that.
So, as I understand it … Is that right?
Yes, I can understand how important it is.

3 Ask for more information, show understanding, and check satisfaction.
And how long have you had this problem?
Could you tell me …?
Does that sound all right?

4 Make promises and keep them, and show follow-up and follow-through.
I'll call you back in half an hour.
I'll call you when … to make sure everything went well.
I'll flag your order as urgent.

5 Ask if the customer needs anything more, and thank the customer.
Can I assist you with anything else today?
Can I help you with anything else?
Thank you for your order.

Exercise 4
1 c 2 e 3 a 4 g 5 f 6 b 7 d

Exercise 5
1 May I help you?
2 Could you give me your customer number, please?
3 I'd just like to confirm your contact details.
4 OK, let me just repeat that.
5 Yes, that's right.
6 could I go over your order again?
7 Can I help you with anything else?

Exercise 6
Answers will vary.

Exercise 7
Possible answers
1 Hello, Mr. Norman. How can I help you today?
2 Would that be our latest accounting software package?
3 Have you ordered from us before?
4 OK, could you give me your customer number, please?
5 Thank you. OK, how many packages would you like to order?
6 OK, could you give me your address, please?
7 Can I help you with anything else?
8 You should receive it by … Thank you for your order.

Exercise 8
Product: i-go mini

Problem: The customer isn't able to install the software.

Action taken: The operator identifies the problem and talks the customer through the steps necessary to resolve it.

So, what exactly is the problem?
Could you explain what you've done so far?
That means you need to have …
Let me just talk you through the steps.
By the way, have you registered with us?

Exercise 9
1 C 2 B 3 A 4 B 5 A 6 B 7 A 8 A 9 C 10 C
11 B 12 A 13 A 14 B

Exercise 10
1 clarify 2 follow 3 explain 4 means 5 stand 6 what
7 talk

Exercise 11
1 Have you tried 2 How about 3 I'd recommend
4 Why don't you

Exercise 12
Answers will vary.

Exercise 13
1 b 2 b 3 a 4 b 5 c 6 a

Exercise 14
Answers will vary.

Warmer
Possible answers
1 Answers will vary.
2 Business contacts and people you don't know well.
3 Close colleagues, friends, and family
4 Answers will vary.
5 In an informal style

Exercise 1
A I B F C F D I

Exercise 2
1 long / uncontracted 2 I'm 3 formal 4 subject
5 formal 6 formal 7 help 8 Let me know if you need any other help

Exercise 3
Dear Mr. Vogt: 1 B 2 F 3 A 4 D
Hi Manfred: 1 E 2 C 3 H 4 G

Exercise 4
1 Dear / Hello / Hi 2 regard 3 Thanks
4 delighted, inform 5 happy, tell 6 other / further
7 me know 8 Kind 9 All

Exercise 5
1 Dear 2 I was pleased 3 I am delighted 4 assist
5 I have attached 6 I would be grateful 7 I will call
8 If you have any further questions, please do not hesitate to contact me 9 I am looking forward 10 Sincerely yours

Exercise 6
1 Dear / Hi 2 glad 3 I'm 4 Let's set up
5 I'll let you know 6 Looking 7 regards / wishes

Exercise 7
Answers will vary.

Exercise 8

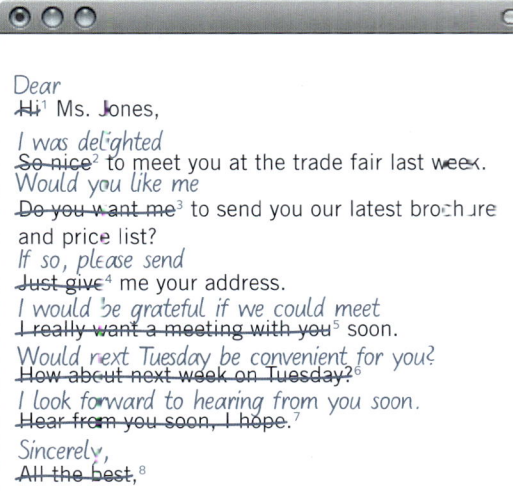

Dear
~~Hi~~[1] Ms. Jones,

I was delighted
~~So nice~~[2] to meet you at the trade fair last week.
Would you like me
~~Do you want me~~[3] to send you our latest brochure and price list?
If so, please send
~~Just give~~[4] me your address.
I would be grateful if we could meet
~~I really want a meeting with you~~[5] soon.
Would next Tuesday be convenient for you?
~~How about next week on Tuesday?~~[6]
I look forward to hearing from you soon.
~~Hear from you soon, I hope.~~[7]
Sincerely,
~~All the best,~~[8]

Mark Elliot

Exercise 9
Possible answer

Dear Joan,

Thank you for your email.

We would be pleased to be able to help you find an apartment in Berlin.

Yes, we can also recommend a place to lease a car. I have attached a list of car dealerships that lease cars.

You will also find information on our service fees attached.

I will give you a call to schedule a time and date to meet. I am looking forward to meeting you and to helping you find a new home in Berlin.

Best regards,

Marcus Schaffer

Exercise 10
1 as soon as possible 2 for your information
3 by the way 4 regarding 5 meeting 6 tomorrow
7 your/you are 8 manager 9 forward 10 please

Exercise 11
1 F 2 F 3 T 4 F 5 T

Exercise 12
Possible answers

Hi Jack,

Regarding our meeting tomorrow, are you talking about the customer survey results? Please let me know.

Best,
Catherine

Hi Catherine,

Yes, I'll talk about the results. By the way, the manager is happy with the feedback!

Best,
Jack

Exercise 13
Possible answers

Hi Gudrun, Thx 4 mtg with me. Will f/u on points. Have questions? Just ask. Best, Jon

Hello Til, Nice 2 c u. Keep in touch! Look fwd to it. Susan

Unit 7

Warmer
Answers will vary.

Exercise 1
a 1 b 5 c 2 d 3 e 7 f 4 g 8 h 6

Exercise 2
1 annoyed 2 shout 3 condescending 4 fault
5 mistake 6 apologize 7 policy 8 resolve

Exercise 3
A Dialogue 3 B Dialogue 1 C Dialogue 2

	Complaint	Response
Dialogue 1	Poor service at bank	Apologizes for service at bank and invites customer into the office to talk without interruption
Dialogue 2	Flight has been canceled	Explains reason for cancellation and offers help
Dialogue 3	Customer has been overcharged	Offers to refund money and agrees to exchange the sweater

Exercise 4
1 seems, problem 2 sorry, hear 3 let me apologize
4 understand 5 inconvenienced 6 let me see, assist
7 appears, mistake 8 refund 9 problem, be glad

Exercise 5
1 It appears as if our information is right.
2 I'm afraid my colleague wasn't to blame for your not having received the order.
3 It seems the company didn't put all the parts in the shipment.
4 It seems I didn't receive your email.
5 I'm afraid you won't get the order this week.

Exercise 6
1 troubled 2 lodge 3 seemed 4 terribly 5 follow
6 Would you mind 7 make sure 8 inconvenienced
9 I'll be glad 10 repeat

Exercise 7
1 I'd like to say how terribly sorry I am. / We really apologize for the poor service.
2 I can understand how this must have ruined your stay with us. So, if I follow you correctly, you had to phone each day to get your room serviced? Would you mind giving me some details?
3 Mr. Smith, I've just spoken to housekeeping.
4 Since you have been so inconvenienced by this incident, I'll be glad to offer you two free nights for your next visit at our hotel.

Exercise 8
1 a 2 c 3 e 4 h 5 j 6 g 7 f 8 i 9 b 10 d

Exercise 9
1 terribly 2 has put 3 oversight 4 resolved 5 follow up
6 make sure 7 compensation 8 inconvenience
9 satisfied 10 hesitate

Exercise 10
1st part: Answers will vary.
2nd part: 1 b 2 e 3 d 4 c 5 a

Exercise 11
Answers will vary.

Exercise 12
Answers will vary.

Phrases to Use

The phrases below will be useful tools in your work. Highlight phrases that are particularly relevant to you, and look at them regularly to help you remember them.

Unit 2

Basic Socializing

Greetings and Introductions

Good morning. You must be …
How do you do? → How do you do?
How are you? → Fine, thanks. And you?
It's nice to finally meet you face-to-face.
    → It's good / nice to meet you, too.
I'd like you to meet …
Have you met …?
Anke, this is …
I'd like to introduce you to …
May I introduce myself? I'm … → Nice to meet
    you. I'm …

Small Talk Questions

How was your trip / flight / drive?
Did you find us OK?
Did you have any trouble finding us?

Is this your first time in Hamburg?
So, have you ever been to Hamburg before?

So, where are you staying?
How's your hotel?

Great weather, isn't it?
How was the weather in New York?
What was the weather like in Houston?

What do you do?
What line of work are you in?

Where do you come from?
Where are you from originally?
What's your hometown like?

What do you do in your free time?
Oh, are you interested in …?

Have you heard about the latest …?

Offering Hospitality

May I take your coat?
Let me help you with that. → Oh, that's very kind
    of you.
So, if you would like to take a seat …
Please take a seat. → Thank you.
Would you care for coffee or tea?
Would you like some coffee or tea? → Yes, please.
    Tea would be nice.
Can I get you some mineral water?
Can I get you something else?

Saying Goodbye

Thanks for coming by.
Thank you for a good meeting.
It was great to meet (both of) you.
Have a good trip.
See you next time.
I look forward to seeing you …
Goodbye. / Bye.

Meeting a Customer at a Trade Fair

Starting a Conversation

Excuse me, may I help you? → No, thanks. I'm just looking / browsing.

How can I help you?

May I introduce myself? I'm … → Nice / Pleased to meet you. I'm …

Could I ask your name? → My name's …

How are you enjoying the fair? → I find it very interesting. It's a good chance to network.

Talking Business

Are you looking for anything special / in particular? → I'm looking for / interested in …

Could I offer you / interest you in …? → Yes, I'd like to have your latest …

Please feel free to ask me any questions.

Would you mind if I call / email / contact you? → No, not all. I look forward to hearing from you.

May I give you my card? → Thank you, here's mine.

Ending a Conversation

It was so nice to meet you.

I hope you enjoy the fair. → Thanks, it was a pleasure. I appreciate your help.

Telephoning

Identifying Yourself (When You Receive a Call)

Good morning. Apex industries.

Hello, Martha Greer speaking. How can / may I help you?

Identifying Yourself (When You Make a Call)

Hello, my name is … I'm with ABC AG in Bonn.

This is Joan Everts from Everts, Samuels, and Barker.

Hello, I'd like to introduce myself.

I'm calling to …

Getting Through

I'd like to speak to John, please.

Could you put me through to John, please?
→ Of course, one moment, please.
→ Thanks for holding. I'm putting you through to John's office now.

Giving Bad News

I'm afraid she's in a meeting right now.

I'm sorry, but the manager is on another line.

Unfortunately, he's out of the office today.

It seems that she's not at / away from her desk.

Taking and Leaving Messages

Would you like to leave a message? → That's OK. I'll call back later.

Could you ask her to call me back as soon as possible? → Yes, I'll make sure she gets your message right away.

I'll make sure he calls you back today.

Difficulty Understanding

Sorry, could you speak up a bit? I can barely / hardly hear you.

Please speak a bit slower / more slowly.

Could you speak a bit softer?

Showing Attention

I'll just write / jot that down.

Let me just make a note of that.

I've got your customer file right in front of me.

I'm checking your file as we speak.

Confirming Information

Can I just go over / confirm the details again?

Let's go over it again to be sure of the details.

Explaining Action

I'll be glad to send this out to you today.

You should receive it by …

Showing Follow-Up

I'll check on that information with my colleague and call you back in two hours.

I'll make sure he/she calls you back today.

I assure you we will contact you on Friday.

Finishing a Call

Can I help / assist you with anything else today?
Can I take care of anything else for you?
Is there anything else I can help you with today?
I appreciate your taking the time to talk with me.
Look forward to hearing from you / speaking to you again soon.
Thanks for calling us.

Making Arrangements

Asking for an Appointment

Could we schedule / fix / set up an appointment?
Are you available / free on Monday?
Is Monday convenient for you?
Does next Thursday suit you?
How / What about 2:00 p.m. on Tuesday?

Agreeing On a Time

Just let me check my diary / planner / calendar.
Yes, Tuesday is fine with me.
Sounds good. Tuesday at 2:00 p.m., then.

Suggesting a New Time

I'm sorry, but I've got another appointment then.
Sorry, I'm tied up on Wednesday.
How about Tuesday morning instead?
Actually, Tuesday afternoon would work out / be better for me.

Confirming

OK, we'll see each other next Thursday at 11:00 a.m. at your office.
Could you confirm the details in an email?
Here's my cell phone number in case you need to reach me.
I look forward to seeing you (then).

Apologizing / Rescheduling

Sorry, I can't make the meeting on Wednesday. Something has come up.
Unfortunately, I can't attend / come.
Could we postpone the meeting until Monday?

Call Center Telephoning

Offering Assistance

How can I help you today?
What can I do for you?

Understanding Customers

I see. So, as I understand it, … Is that correct?
Let me just repeat that.

Troubleshooting

What seems to be the problem?
Could you explain the problem in more detail?
Please tell me what you've done so far.
Let me talk you through the steps.
Do you follow / understand me so far?
Please let me know if something isn't clear.

Confirming Details

Could I just have your name and address, please?
I'd just like to confirm your contact details.
Could I go over your order again?

Making Promises and Keeping Them

Your order will go out overnight today.
I'll call you back in half an hour.
I will personally make sure …

Agreeing on Action and Ensuring Satisfaction

Does that sound all right?
Do you have any other questions?
I hope this is to your satisfaction.

Following Up and Following Through

I'll call you to make sure everything is all right

Formal and Informal Business Writing

*   The texts in pink should only be used in informal writing.

Salutations and Closings
Dear Mr. Schmidt,
Sincerely (yours),
Harold Jones

Dear Sirs / Sir or Madam,
Yours faithfully,
Thomas Hanson

Hello / Hi Jörg,
Best wishes, / All the best, / Take care,
Barbara

Connecting with a Reader
In reference to your letter / email of January 3 …
In regards to your phone call …
Further to our recent meeting …
Re your letter / email of …
Thanks for your phone call this morning.
I hope everything is going well.

Stating the Reason for Writing
We are writing to confirm …
I am writing to let you know …
I would like to inform you …
I'm just writing to tell you …
I'd like to let you know …
Just a quick email to let you know …

Enclosures (for Letters Only)
Please find enclosed the price list you requested.
In the enclosed information packet, you will find …
As you will see from the enclosed brochure, …

Attachments (for Emails Only)
I am sending you … as an attachment.
I have attached the … as a PDF.
Please see the attached …
Please complete the attached form and return it
    to us.

Giving Good News
We are pleased to say …
I am delighted to inform you …
I'm happy to tell you …
I'm glad to tell you …

Giving Bad News
I am afraid / Unfortunately, I must inform you …
We regret to inform you …
Got bad news for you.
Sorry to say …

Making Requests
We would be grateful if we could …
I would appreciate it if we could …
It'd be great if we could …
Could you … ?

Taking Action
I will call you / contact you …
We would be delighted / pleased to assist you.
I'll get in touch with you / get back to you …
I'd be glad to help out.

Concluding
If you have any further questions, please do not
    hesitate to contact me.
If you have any other questions, please contact me.
We look forward to hearing from / meeting you
    soon.
I look forward to seeing you next week.
Let me know if you need anything else / any other
    help.
Look(ing) forward to your reply / to hearing from
    you.
Look(ing) forward to seeing you next week.

Problems and Complaints

Apologizing

First of all, I'm so / terribly sorry about that.
I apologize for …
We regret hearing about …

Clarifying Information

Could you tell me exactly what happened?
Could you explain a bit more …?
Would you mind if I just went over that again?

Listening Carefully

I'll just make a few notes as you speak.
I'm just taking this down.

Showing Empathy

I understand.
I see what you mean.
I would feel the same way.
I see exactly the reason for your complaint.
What a difficult situation this puts you in.

Taking Responsibility

There seems be a misunderstanding.
It appears your order got overlooked.
I'm afraid there has been some sort of mix-up.
It looks like an oversight on our part.
It seems (that) the order was not handled promptly
    enough.
It appears (that) a mistake has been made.

Saying How and When a Problem Will Be Solved

I'll take care of this for you at once.
I'll get back to you right away.
You'll receive a refund / replacement by tomorrow.
I'm sure we can find a solution.
I'd be glad to offer you … to make up for this
    inconvenience.
This should be resolved by the end of today.

Offering an Alternative

If this solution does not meet your needs, then
    I can suggest … as an alternative.
I'll look into other possibilities by …

Summarizing a Discussion

What we have decided is …
Our action plan is …
I'd like to go over this once more to make sure
    we agree.

Assuring a Customer of Follow-Up

I'll get back to you in / by …
I'll follow up to make sure that …

Ending with a Friendly, Helpful Tone

I hope you are satisfied with the outcome.
Thanks for bringing this to our attention.
Is there anything else I can help you with today?
Don't hesitate to call again if there are any more
    problems.

Dealing with Complaints in Writing (Formal)

We very much regret …
We are very concerned to hear that …
We assure you that we are doing everything
    we can.
The problem has now been resolved.
Once again, we apologize for the inconvenience.
We do value your business and hope to keep you
    as a long-term customer.

A–Z Wordlist

A

ability Fähigkeit
access Zugriff
accommodation Unterkunft
according to nach, gemäß
account Konto
to **admit** zugeben
advice Rat
to **affect s.o./sth.** jmd./etw.
  beeinflussen
to **alienate s.o.** jmd. vor den Kopf
  stoßen, abschrecken
annoyed verärgert
to **apologize** sich entschuldigen
appointment Termin,
  Verabredung
to **appreciate sth.** etw. zu
  schätzen wissen
appropriate angemessen
arrangement Absprache
to **assess** beurteilen, bemessen
to **assume** vermuten
to **assure** versichern
at ease entspannt
to **attend** teilnehmen
attention Aufmerksamkeit
attentive aufmerksam
attitude Einstellung
attrition Verschleiß, Verlust
available verfügbar
awful furchtbar

B

to **be in charge of s.o./
  sth.** Verantwortung für jmd./
  etw. tragen
to **be responsible for (doing)
  sth.** für etw. zuständig sein
benefit Nutzen, Vorteil
to **blame s.o.** jmd. Vorwürfe
  machen
to **boost** fördern, steigern
to **bother** stören
to **browse sth.** etw. durchstöbern
busy besetzt
buzz phrase Schlagwort

C

to **calm s.o.** jmd. beruhigen
certainly sicher, zweifellos
challenge Herausforderung
clarification Klärung,
  Verdeutlichung
to **clear** gutschreiben
clerk Angestellte/r, Beamte/r
to **come across** auf andere wirken

to **come up** dazwischen kommen
commitment Verpflichtung
company Unternehmen
compared (to) verglichen (mit)
compensation Entschädigung
competitor Konkurrent,
  Mitbewerber
complaint Beschwerde
complimentary gratis
comprehension Verständnis
condescending herablassend
to **conduct** betreiben,
  durchführen
confidence Selbstvertrauen
confined begrenzt
to **confirm** bestätigen
connection Verbindung
constantly ständig
contact details Kontaktdaten
contentment Zufriedenheit
contract Vertrag
convenient günstig, praktisch
courtesy Höflichkeit
to **crave** sich sehnen nach
crucial ausschlaggebend
current aktuell
customer Kunde/Kundin
to **cut off** eine Verbindung
  trennen

D

to **damage sth.** etw. schaden
database Datenbank
dated veraltet, überholt
to **deal with sth.** sich mit etw.
  befassen/auseinandersetzten
to **decide** entscheiden
to **decipher** entschlüsseln
delay Verspätung
delicious lecker, delikat
delighted erfreut
demand Nachfrage, Bedarf
to **depend on s.o./sth.** von
  jmd./etw. abhängen
to **describe** beschreiben
to **detect** erfassen, erkennen
to **develop** entwickeln
directory Telefonverzeichnis
to **discover** entdecken
to **dismiss sth.** etw. abtun
to **dispatch** abschicken

E

to **ease** lindern
efficiency Effizienz
empathy Einfühlungsvermögen

encounter Treffen
essentials Wesentliche
to **establish** aufbauen, (Kontakt)
  herstellen
exchange Umtausch
expense Ausgabe
experience Erfahrung
extension Durchwahl

F

familiar bekannt, vertraut
fault Schuld
to **flag** markieren
to **follow through** etw. zu Ende
  führen
forgiveness Nachsicht,
  Vergebung
foundation Basis, Fundament
free of charge kostenlos

G

generous großzügig
genuine authentisch, echt
to **get back to s.o.** jmd.
  antworten
glad froh
to **go over sth.** etw. durchsehen
going-away party Ausstand
grateful dankbar
to **greet s.o.** jmd. begrüßen
to **grow up** aufwachsen

H

to **handle sth.** sich mit etw.
  befassen, etw. handhaben
handy griffbereit
hardly kaum, schwer
to **have had it** die Nase voll
  haben, etw. satt haben
to **hesitate** zögern
hospitality Gastfreundlichkeit
**Human Resources
  (HR)** Personalabteilung

I

impact Auswirkung, Einfluss
improvement Verbesserung
incident Zwischenfall
to **inconvenience s.o.** jmd.
  Umstände bereiten
to **increase** erhöhen
indifference Gleichgültigkeit
to **influence** beeinflussen
to **initiate sth.** etw. anfangen,
  einleiten
inquiry Anfrage
to **interact** interagieren

internship Praktikum, Praxissemester
to **interrupt** unterbrechen
to **introduce s.o./yourself** jmd./ sich vorstellen
to **invite** einladen
issue Problem, Thema

J
to **join s.o.** sich zu jmd. gesellen
to **jot sth. down** etw. notieren

K
kind freundlich, nett
knowledgeable sachkundig

L
to **lack** mangeln
to **launch** starten, beginnen
line Leitung
line of business Branche
to **lodge** einreichen

M
to **maintain sth.** etw. aufrecht erhalten
manner Art, Weise
to **measure** messen, abschätzen
memorized auswendig gelernt
mind Gedanke, Verstand
to **mind sth.** etw. dagegen haben
to **mingle** sich unter die Leute mischen
monitored überwacht

N
to **notice** bemerken

O
obvious offensichtlich
to **occur** vorkommen, stattfinden
to **offer** anbieten
on hold in der telefonischen Warteschleife
order entry clerk Angestellte/r in der Auftragserfassung
originally ursprünglich
overbearing überheblich
to **overcharge** zu viel berechnen
to **overlook** überblicken
oversight Versehen

P
patient geduldig
to **pencil in** mit Bleistift eintragen, vorläufig vormerken
permission Erlaubnis
pitch Verkaufstechnik, Tonhöhe
to **place (an order)** (eine Bestellung) aufgeben
pleased zufrieden, hoch erfreut
pleasant angenehm

pointless zwecklos
policy Politik, Grundsatz
polite höflich
to **postpone sth.** etw. verlegen, aufschieben
to **prefer** bevorzugen
to **prepare** vorbereiten
pressure Druck
to **presume** annehmen
principle Grundlage, Richtlinie
product range Sortiment, Produktpalette
promise Versprechen
to **promote sth.** für etw. werben
to **prompt** anregen, der Anlass für etwas sein
to **provide** bieten
to **purchase** kaufen
to **put through** durchstellen

Q
to **quote** anbieten

R
to **rank** rangieren
rapport gutes Verhältnis
rare selten
to **rate** bewerten
rationale Gründe
to **reach s.o.** jmd. erreichen
reason Grund
to **recall sth.** sich an etw. erinnern
receipt Beleg
to **receive** erhalten
reception desk Empfangsschalter, Rezeption
recipient Empfänger
to **recommend** empfehlen
to **refund** erstatten
to **regret** bedauern
to **repeat** wiederholen
to **require** benötigen
to **reschedule sth.** etw. verschieben, neu planen
to **resolve sth.** etw. beheben
response Reaktion, Antwort
responsibility Verantwortung
rude unhöflich
to **rush** beschleunigen, antreiben

S
sales Vertrieb
sales rep (representative) Außendienstmitarbeiter/in, Vertreter/in
satisfaction Zufriedenstellung
to **score** erzielen
to **set up a meeting** ein Meeting anberaumen/abhalten

sincere aufrichtig
skill Fertigkeit
sloppy nachlässig, schludrig
to **solve (a problem)** ein Problem lösen
to **speak up** lauter sprechen
to **stand** ausstehen
step Schritt
stock Bestand, Vorrat
stuck festsitzen
successful erfolgreich
succinct bündig, prägnant
to **suggest** behaupten, vorschlagen
suitable passend
to **summarize** zusammenfassen
superior ausgezeichnet
supervisor Vorgesetzte/r, Aufseher/in
survey Umfrage
to **switch off** abschalten
system requirement Systemanforderung

T
tact Taktgefühl
target Ziel, Vorgabe
teller Bankkassierer/in
thirsty durstig
tied up beschäftigt
tool Instrument, Arbeitshilfe
topic Thema
to **track** (nach)verfolgen
trade fair (Handels-)Messe
traffic jam Stau
transfer Überweisung
to **treat s.o. (in a certain way)** jmd. (auf eine bestimmte Art und Weise) behandeln
tricky heikel, knifflig
trouble Problem, Schwierigkeit
trust Vertrauen
turnover Fluktuation
to **type** tippen

U
to **underestimate** unterschätzen
underpaid unterbezahlt
urgent dringend

V
valued geschätzt
voucher Gutschein

W
weight Gewicht
willingness Bereitwilligkeit
to **wrap up sth.** etw. beenden

Z
zip code Postleitzahl

Tracklist

Track	Title	Exercise	Running time
01	Title/Copyright		0:55
02	Unit 1	Exercise 8	1:10
03	Unit 1	Exercise 10	1:36
04	Unit 2	Exercise 3	1:02
05	Unit 2	Exercise 7	0:32
06	Unit 2	Exercise 13	1:29
07	Unit 3	Exercise 2	2:07
08	Unit 3	Exercise 7	1:19
09	Unit 3	Exercise 10	1:50
10	Unit 3	Exercise 14	1:14
11	Unit 4	Exercise 1	1:39
12	Unit 4	Exercise 2	2:31
13	Unit 4	Exercise 10	1:09
14	Unit 4	Exercise 13	0:42
15	Unit 5	Exercise 1	4:04
16	Unit 5	Exercise 5	1:37
17	Unit 5	Exercise 6	1:04
18	Unit 5	Exercise 8	3:00
19	Unit 5	Exercise 11	1:14
20	Unit 6	Exercise 11	3:28
21	Unit 7	Exercise 1	1:31
22	Unit 7	Exercise 3	2:14
23	Unit 7	Exercise 6	1:55
Total running time			39:24

Aufnahmestudio: New York Audio Productions